U0084982

序 言

　　商場如戰場，除了要「**快**」、要「**準**」之外，擁有**良好的英語會話技巧**，更是商場上致勝的主要利器。我們特針對讀者的需求，傾全力編著了這本「**商用基礎會話**」（ *Business Talks in English* ）。

　　本書共十二章，五十二個單元。內容涵蓋最廣，從造訪、詢問、參觀工廠、產品介紹、商談、訂貨…到簽約、議價、索賠等。並以各個單元為主題，衍生出各種不同的商談狀況，共計兩百多個狀況。更以斜黑字體標示出各個狀況最重要的句子，使您一目了然，背起來輕鬆，用起來容易。而在每個unit（單元）前，列有「**對話精華**」，那更是您成功致勝的關鍵句，切題好用，便於背誦。每課之後，為您詳列了重要的單字、片語，使您在分秒必爭的商務競爭中，能省却查字典的麻煩。

　　From conversation to communication，會話的目的在於溝通。「**商用基礎會話**」所採用的句子，句句簡明扼要，各個商談狀況更是精彩活潑，讀了就會運用。

　　審慎的編校是我們一貫的原則，倘有疏漏之處，尚祈各界先進不吝批評指教。

編者 謹識

CONTENTS

CHAPTER **1** 預訂約會・造訪基礎會話

CHAPTER **2** 參觀工廠基礎會話

CHAPTER **3** 詢問・徵信基礎會話

CHAPTER **4** 談論公司基礎會話

商用基礎會話

BUSINESS TALKS IN ENGLISH

商用基礎會話　BUSINESS TALKS IN ENGLISH

CHAPTER 10 商業交易實況會話

CHAPTER 11 商場應對實況會話

CHAPTER 12 公司業務實況會話

商用基礎會話
BUSINESS TALKS IN ENGLISH

預訂約會・造訪
基礎會話

CHAPTER I

1. 如何預訂約會
2. 會面時的應對

UNIT 1

How to set an appointment
如何預訂約會

＜對話精華＞

· What time **would be convenient** for you？
  什麼時候您方便呢？

· Any time you say. 您說什麼時候都可以。

· We'll be **expecting** you. 我們將期待您的到來。

※ 希望會面時 ※

■ I'd like to **make an appointment** to see you.　　　　我想約個時間見您。

■ I'd like to come and see you.　　　　我想去見您。

■ Would it be possible for me to talk to you **in person** about that？　　　　我能不能和您本人談談那件事？

■ I'd like to see you at your earliest possible convenience.　　　　如果方便的話，我想儘早去見您。

■ Could we **get together** and discuss it a little more？　　　　我們能不能聚在一起，再多討論一點這件事？

＊＊

in person 親自；本人　　*at one's convenience* 在方便的時候
get together 聚會

■ Could we meet and discuss the matter in a little more detail?　　我們能不能碰個面，再多討論一點這件事的細節？

■ *I wonder* if it would be possible for us to meet at your earliest convenience and discuss the matter in a little more detail.　　如果方便的話，不知道我們能不能儘早和您見面，再多討論一點這件事的細節。

■ Could I see Mr. Booth sometime this week?　　我能不能在這個禮拜的哪個時候，見見布斯先生？

■ Should I visit you, or would you like to come over here and see our setup?　　我應該去拜訪您，或者是您要到這裏來，看看我們的機械裝置？

■ Would you like to come to my office?　　您要不要來我的辦公室？

※ 詢問對方方便的時間 ※

■ *What time would be convenient for you*?　　什麼時候您方便呢？

■ When is it convenient for you?　　什麼時候您方便呢？

■ When would it be most convenient for you?　　什麼時候您最方便呢？

■ When can we meet to talk?　　我們什麼時候可以見面談一談？

** wonder〔'wʌndɚ〕*v.* 想曉得；極欲知道　　setup〔'sɛt,ʌp〕*n.* 機械裝置

❈ 方便與不方便的時候 ❈

▨ Please **call on** me when it is convenient for you.   請在您方便的時候來找我。

▨ Please call on me anytime it suits you.   請在任何您方便的時候來找我。

▧ ***Any time you say***.   您說什麼時候都可以。

▨ Any time between three and five.   三點到五點之間的任何時間都可以。

▨ ***I'm free after*** three o'clock.   三點以後,我就有空了。

▨ I'll be out of town tomorrow, but almost anytime after that would be fine with me.   明天我將出城到外地去,不過,之後的任何時間,我幾乎都可以。

▨ ***I'm expecting*** some visitors tomorrow morning.   明天早上,我要等幾個訪客來。

▨ I'm afraid I'm busy all day tomorrow.   恐怕明天一天,我都很忙。

▨ I'm sorry, I have an appointment.   抱歉,我有個約會。

---

call on *sb.* 短暫地訪問某人   **suit** 〔sjut〕*v.* 適合於;對~方便

expect 〔ɪk'spɛkt〕*v.* 期待(其後接受詞,若不接受詞則為「懷孕」之意,應特別注意其用法)

❋ 約定拜訪時間 ❋

▓ I'd like to meet you at three o'clock in the afternoon. | 我想下午三點的時候跟您見面。

▓ I'd like to see you tomorrow if you have time. | 如果您有時間，我想明天去見您。

▓ **How about** tomorrow at ten？ | 明天十點怎麼樣？

▓ How about the day after tomorrow？ | 後天怎麼樣？

▓ How about eleven o'clock in my office？ | 十一點在我的辦公室怎麼樣？

▓ Could we make a **tentative appointment** for, say, Thursday at two o'clock？ | 我們能不能暫時約在，嗯，星期四兩點？

▓ **Are you free** next Tuesday at two o'clock？ | 下星期二兩點你有空嗎？

▓ Is that convenient for you？ | 那個時間您方不方便？

▓ I'll see you at eleven. | 十一點見。

❋ 期待訪客光臨 ❋

▓ **We'll be expecting you.** | 我們將期待您的到來。

▓ We'll be waiting for you. | 我們將等著您來。

---

tentative〔ˈtɛntətɪv〕*adj.* 暫時性的　　**wait for** 等候；期待

■ I'm looking forward to meeting you.　　我期待與您見面。

■ See you soon.　　　　　　　　　　再見。

❋ 有事的話請打電話來 ❋

■ Please call me again to let me
know when you're coming.
　　您要來時，請再打通電話
告訴我。

■ *If you have* any problem, just
call and let me know.
　　如果您有任何問題，就打
電話來告訴我。

■ If you have any trouble, give
me a call.
　　如果您有任何困難，打個
電話給我。

■ In case you have any trouble,
call me.
　　萬一您有任何困難，打電
話給我。

❋ 告訴訪客如何到自己的公司 ❋

■ *How do I get to* your office?　　我怎麼到您的公司呢？

■ Could you tell me how to get to
your office?
　　能不能告訴我，怎麼到您
的公司？

■ *How will you be coming*, by taxi
or by bus?
　　您會怎麼來？搭計程車還
是公車？

■ The taxi is *the fastest way to come*.　　搭計程車來最快。

**

look forward to 期望；盼望　　*in case* 如果；萬一　　*get to* 到達

▨ We're not far from Central Bank of China.

我們這兒離中央銀行不遠。

▨ Our office is just *a short walk from* the Taipei City Council.

我們公司離台北市議會，只有一小段路程。

▨ Do you know how to get to the Taipei Station by bus?

您知道怎麼搭公車到台北火車站嗎？

▨ Do you know how to go to the Ministry of Audit?

您知道怎麼去審計部嗎？

▨ *Do you understand the way to the* Ministery of Education?

您知道到教育部的路嗎？

▨ Do you know the Taipei Hilton Hotel?

您知不知道台北希爾頓飯店？

▨ Our company is in a building near the Taipei Hilton Hotel.

我們公司就在台北希爾頓飯店附近的一座建築物裏。

▨ Go out the south exit of Taipei Station.

走出台北火車站的南邊出口。

▨ When you go out the south exit, *make a right turn* and go about fifty meters.

當你一走出南邊出口，向右轉再走大約五十公尺。

---

council〔'kaʊnsl̩〕*n.* 議會　　audit〔'ɔdɪt〕*n.* 帳目稽核

exit〔'ɛkzɪt〕*n.* 出口　　meter〔'mitɚ〕*n.* 公尺；米

▓ ***Turn to the right*** at the inter-
section and you'll see a ***highrise***
in front of you.

在十字路口向右轉，您就會
看到一棟高樓在您的面前。

▓ Turn right at the second in-
tersection and you'll see the
Duke Building on your left.

在第二個十字路口向右轉，
您就會看到公爵大廈在您的
左側。

▓ Our office is on the tenth
floor.

我們公司在十樓。

▓ ***Get*** a taxi and ***ask for*** the
Ambassador Mansion on Sec. 4
Chung Hsiao E. Rd. and the
driver will understand.

叫一輛計程車，說要到忠孝
東路四段上的國賓大廈，司
機就知道了。

※ 更改拜訪的時間 ※

▓ I'm afraid I have to ***cancel***
our appointment.

恐怕我必須取消我們的約會。

▓ I'm afraid I'll have to ***post-
pone*** our appointment.

恐怕我必須將我們的約會延
期。

▓ ***Something's come up***. Can we
make our appointment a little
later ?

發生了一點事情，我們可不
可以把約會延一下？

---

intersection〔͵ɪntəˈsɛkʃən〕*n.* 十字路口
highrise〔ˈhaɪ͵raɪz〕*n.* 多層建築物；高樓　　cancel〔ˈkænsḷ〕*v.* 取消
postpone〔postˈpon〕*v.* 延期

▓ Something urgent has happened.
I won't be able to *make it* this
afternoon.

發生了緊急的事，下午我不能夠赴約。

▓ I have to go to Kaohsiung tomorrow morning.

我明早必須去高雄。

▓ I may be a little late but please
wait for me.

我也許會慢一點，不過請你等我。

▓ That's all right.

沒關係。

▓ Would you like to *reschedule* the
appointment ?

您要不要重新約個時間？

▓ Would you like to decide on another time ?

您要不要另外決定個時間？

▓ How about Thursday at the same
time ?

星期四同一個時間怎麼樣？

▓ How does Friday at the same
time *sound* to you ?

星期五同一個時間，您覺得如何？

** ────────────────────

urgent〔'ɜdʒnt〕*adj.* 緊急的   *make it* 達成某項特定目標
decide on 決定

UNIT 2

Reception
會面時的應對

<対話精華>

· I hope you didn't have any trouble finding us.
　希望您找到我們，並沒有什麼困難。

· *How's everything with you* ? 您近況如何呢？

· I'm looking forward to meeting you again (soon).
　我期盼（很快）再見到您。

❋ 打電話告訴對方您已抵達 ❋

◼ I've just come from Taipei. 　　　　我剛剛從台北來。

◼ I've just arrived in New York. 　　我剛剛抵達紐約。

◼ I just called to *let* you *know*　　我只是打電話來告訴您，
　I've arrived. 　　　　　　　　　　　我已經到了。

❋ 接到訪客抵達的電話 ❋

◼ I've been expecting your call. 　　我一直等著您的電話。

◼ When did you come ? 　　　　　　您什麼時候來的？

**
arrive〔ə'raɪv〕*v.* 抵達某地　　　*let know* 告訴；通知

▓ When did you *get in* ? 您什麼時候到的？

▓ *It's nice to know* you got here safely. 知道您平安抵達，眞好。

▓ Can we do anything for you ? 有什麼我們能爲您效勞的嗎？

✳ 說明來訪的對象 ✳

▓ Good morning. My name is Ta-Jen Liu. *I'm here to* meet Mr. Barber. 早，我叫劉達人。我來這裏見巴勃先生。

▓ I have an appointment to see Mr. Smith at ten. 我和史密斯先生約定十點見面。

▓ I have an appointment with Mr. Smith. 我和史密斯先生有約。

▓ A : Do you have an appointment, Mr. Chen ?

　B : Yes, I believe Mr. Scott is expecting me.

A：陳先生，你事先約好了嗎？

B：是的，我想史考特先生正在等我。

▓ I *phoned earlier* for an appointment. 我事先打電話約過了。

**
get in 到達　　phone〔fon〕*v.* 打電話

❋ 詢問訪客有沒有迷路 ❋

▓ Did you find us all right ?　　　你是順利找到我們的嗎 ?

▓ A : I hope you *didn't have any*　A : 希望您找到我們，並
　　　trouble finding us.　　　　　　沒有什麼困難。

　　B : No, I didn't have any trouble.　B : 沒有，一點困難都沒
　　　　I didn't get lost.　　　　　　　有，我並沒有迷路。

▓ I trust you didn't have a problem　相信您找到我們，並沒有
finding us.　　　　　　　　　　　什麼問題。

❋ 初次見面的問候語 ❋

▓ *How do you do*, Mr. Smith ?　　您好嗎，史密斯先生 ?

▓ *I'm* Ta-Jen Liu *from* Yue Tai　我是裕台貿易公司的劉達
Trading Company.　　　　　　　人。

▓ I'm Chen-Hua Chao of Pioneer　我是先鋒化工公司的趙振
Chemical Corp.　　　　　　　　華。

▓ *I'm glad to meet you*, Mr. Smith.　很高興見到您，史密斯先生。

▓ I'm very happy to meet you,　很高興見到您，史密斯先生。
Mr. Smith.

▓ I'm very pleased to meet you,　很高興見到您，史密斯先生。
Mr. Smith.

✱✱

lost〔lɔst〕*adj.* 迷途的　　pioneer〔,paɪə'nɪr〕*n.* 先鋒；先驅者

▨ It's a pleasure to meet you, Mr. Smith.　很高興見到您，史密斯先生。

▨ *It's nice to make your acquaintance*, Mr. Smith.　認識您是件愉快的事，史密斯先生。

▨ I've been looking forward to meeting you.　我一直盼望著與您見面。

▨ I've heard a lot about you from Mr. Scott.　我從史考特先生那兒，聽到很多關於您的事。

❋ 對舊識的問候語 ❋

▨ A : Good morning, Mr. Jackson. *How are you*?　A：早，傑克森先生。你好嗎？

　B : Fine, thanks. And you?　B：很好，謝謝。你呢？

▨ (It's) Good to see you again.　很高興再見到你。

▨ (It's) Nice to see you again.　很高興再見到你。

▨ (I'm) Happy to see you again.　很高興再見到你。

▨ *I haven't seen* you for a long time.　好久沒看到你了。

▨ A : *How's everything with you*?　A：你近況如何呢？

　B : Everything's fine, thank you.　B：一切如意，謝謝你。

** ────────────────────

make one's acquaintance 與某人結識

▨ A： How are you doing？ A：你好嗎？
　 B： Fine. Couldn't be better. B：很好，再好不過了。

▨ A： How are things？ A：近況如何？
　 B： Everything's the same. B：一切都是老樣子。

▨ A： ***How's it going***？ A：近況如何？
　 B： Everything's the same ***as usual***. B：一切和往常一樣。

▨ A： How's business？ A：生意怎麼樣？
　 B： It's going well. B：很順利。

▨ A： What's new？ A：有什麼新鮮事？
　 B： Nothing much. How about you？ B：沒什麼。你呢？

▨ A： What's happening？ A：有沒有什麼事？
　 B： Nothing really. How about you？ B：也沒什麼。你呢？

※ 詢問旅途的情況 ※

▨ A： ***How was your trip***？ A：旅途如何？
　 B： It was fine. B：很好。

▨ A： Did you have a good trip？ A：旅途愉快嗎？
　 B： Yes, it was very pleasant. B：是的，非常愉快。

▨ Did you have a good flight？ 航程愉快嗎？

---

as usual 像平常一樣　　flight〔flaɪt〕*n.* 航程

A： Do you have much trouble with *jet lag* ?

A：您有沒有受時差的困擾？

B： No, I don't think jet lag bothers me so much.

B：沒有，我想時差並不太困擾我。

※ **道別時** ※

■ *I'm glad to have met you*, Mr. Smith.

很高興和您見面，史密斯先生。

■ It was very nice meeting you, Mr. Kent.

和您見面真是愉快，肯特先生。

■ *Nice to* have met you, Mr. Scott.

很高興和您見面，史考特先生。

■ I'm looking forward to our next meeting.

我期盼我們下次的會面。

■ I'm looking forward to meeting you again (soon).

我期盼（很快）再見到您。

■ See you in May.

五月再見。

■ I'll see you soon. So long.

很快就會再見到您。再會。

■ Thank you for all of your help.

謝謝您的一切幫助。

■ *Thank you for your time*.

謝謝您花那麼多時間。

＊＊

jet lag 因搭乘快速噴射機旅行，飛越時區所引起的生理節律上之障礙、疲倦、急躁等徵候

██ ***Thank you for everything you did for us*.**　　感謝您為我們所做的一切。

██ Thank you for your trouble.　　謝謝您的辛勞。

██ I hope you have *a nice trip home.*　　希望您歸途愉快。

██ Have a nice trip. Goodbye.　　祝旅途愉快。再見。

██ I hope you will come to Taiwan again sometime.　　希望您有空再到台灣來。

██ Thank you very much for coming all the way to *see* me *off*.　　非常謝謝您老遠來為我送行。

✱✱ ───────────

　　see sb. off　（到機場、車站）送（某人）

參觀工廠
基礎會話

CHAPTER
II

UNIT 1

To invite or ask for a tour of a factory
邀請或要求參觀工廠

<對話精華>

- You'll *understand* our products *better* if you visit the plant. 如果您參觀了工廠，您會更加了解我們的產品。
- Will you *show* me your plant？能帶我參觀你們的工廠嗎？
- *Let's talk about* tomorrow's schedule.
  我們來談談明天的日程表。

※ 邀請訪客到工廠參觀 ※

▓ Won't you visit our plant？　　　您不參觀我們的工廠嗎？

▓ You'll *understand* our products　如果您參觀了工廠，您會
　better if you visit the plant.　更加了解我們的產品。

▓ If you have time please *tour*　如果您有時間，請參觀我
　our plant.　　　　　　　　　　們的工廠。

▓ I *advise* you to see our plant　我建議您親自看看我們的
　with your own eyes.　　　　　　工廠。

**

advise〔əd'vaɪz〕*v.* 建議

❀ 要求參觀工廠 ❀

▨ Will you *show* me your plant？　　能帶我參觀你們的工廠嗎？

▨ If it's possible, I'd like to　　如果可能的話，我想參觀你
visit your plant.　　　　　　　們的工廠。

▨ I'd certainly like to visit your　　我確實想要參觀你們的工廠。
plant.

▨ I'd like to have a look at your　　我想要看一看你們的工廠。
plant.

▨ I wonder if you could *show*　　不知道您是否可以帶我四處
me around.　　　　　　　　　　看看。

❀ 商量行程 ❀

▨ *What about* your schedule？　　您的時間表是怎樣的？

▨ Would you tell me about your　　您能告訴我您的時間表嗎？
schedule？

▨ Shall we discuss the schedule？　　我們要討論一下時間表嗎？

▨ *Let's talk about* tomorrow's　　我們來談談明天的時間表。
schedule.

▨ Here's your schedule.　　　　　　這是您的時間表。

▨ We've arranged your schedule.　　我們已安排好您的時間表。

＊＊─────────────────────

have a look at sth. 看一看（某物）　　schedule〔'skɛdʒʊl〕*n.* 時間表

▨ Will we have time to do all this? 　　我們會有時間做完全部（的參觀）嗎？

▨ I'd like to **pick** you **up** here at eight tomorrow morning. 　　我想明天早上八點來這兒載您。

▨ I'm going to show you around the plant in the morning. 　　早上我將帶您看看工廠。

▨ When we arrive at the plant, I will **give you a tour of** the facilities. 　　等我們到達工廠，我會帶您參觀工廠的設備。

▨ And then we can go out to our **service center.** 　　然後我們可以離開工廠，到我們的服務中心。

▨ Please look at the way we pack and ship. 　　請看我們包裝和裝船的方式。

▨ Please come and visit our laboratory in the afternoon. 　　下午請來參觀我們的實驗室。

▨ We'll have a meeting at two. 　　兩點鐘我們將有一場會議。

▨ A : Who will **attend** the meeting? 　　A：誰將出席會議呢？
　　B : Mr. Wang, Mr. Lee, and I will attend the meeting. 　　B：王先生、李先生和我將會出席會議。

▨ **How long** will the meeting **last**? 　　這個會議要開多久呢？

▨ The meeting will probably be over at five. 　　會議大概是在五點結束。

---

ship〔ʃɪp〕v. 裝載到船上；用船運輸
laboratory〔'læbrə,torɪ〕n. 實驗室　　attend〔ə'tɛnd〕v. 出席

UNIT 2

Before touring a factory
參觀工廠前

＜對話精華＞

· I hope you'll **be satisfied with** everything.
　希望您對一切都將感到滿意。

· Would you like to see our catalog?
　你要不要看看我們的目錄？

· I'd like you to **meet** some of our people.
　我想讓您見見我們公司的一些成員。

※ **參觀工廠前** ※

Thank you for visiting our plant.	謝謝您來參觀我們工廠。
I hope you'll find everything satisfactory.	希望您對一切，都將感到滿意。
I hope you'll **be satisfied with** everything.	希望您對一切，都將感到滿意。
I've been looking forward to seeing your plant.	我一直期待著參觀你們的工廠。

＊＊

satisfactory〔,sætɪs'fæktərɪ〕*adj.* 令人滿意的

I hope to learn a lot from this.	我希望能從這次參觀學到很多。
I hope I'm not disturbing you.	希望我沒有打擾您。

❋ 觀看小冊子及錄影帶等 ❋

Would you like to see our catalog?	您要不要看看我們的目錄？
Shall I show you our catalog?	您需要看看我們的目錄嗎？
May I show you our brochure?	我拿我們的小冊子給您看看好嗎？
Here are our pamphlets.	這是我們的小冊子。
Would you please look on page fifteen of this booklet?	請看這本小冊子的第十五頁好嗎？
Please look on page twenty-five for our yearly production.	請看第二十五頁上，本公司的年度產品。
I'll show you a video introducing our company.	我將讓您看看介紹我們公司的錄影帶。
Would you like to see a video about our plant?	您想看看有關我們工廠的錄影帶嗎？

＊＊—————————

disturb〔dɪ'stɝb〕v. 使困擾　　catalog〔'kætḷ,ɔg〕n. 目錄
brochure〔bro'ʃʊr〕n. 小冊子（＝ pamphlet; booklet）

▓ Please look at this commercial video about our new product.

請看看有關我們新產品的商業錄影帶。

❋ 介紹同事給訪客 ❋

▓ I'd like you to *meet* some of our people.

我想讓您見見我們公司的一些成員。

▓ Mr. Smith, I'd like to introduce Mr. Wang, our president.

史密斯先生,我想向您介紹我們的董事長,王先生。

▓ Mr. Smith, *may I introduce* Mr. Lin, the sales manager.

史密斯先生,容我向您介紹銷售部經理,林先生。

▓ Mr. Smith, let me introduce my colleague, Mr. Lee.

史密斯先生,讓我向您介紹我的同事,李先生。

▓ Mr. Smith, this is Mr. Chen, the plant manager.

史密斯先生,這是工廠經理,陳先生。

▓ On my right is Mr. Chang, the sales engineer.

我的右手邊是銷售工程師,張先生。

❋ 介紹公司的主管給訪客 ❋

▓ Mr. Wang is *in charge of* that sort of thing.

王先生負責那方面的事。

---

colleague〔ˈkɑlig〕*n.* 同事　*in charge of* 負責管理

▓ He's with the product development department.　　他在產品開發部門。

▓ He's in charge of promotion and public relations.　　他負責促銷和公共關係。

▓ He's been to the United States several times.　　他曾到過美國好幾次。

▓ He *was promoted to* chief of the overseas sales department last year.　　去年他被擢陞爲海外銷售部主管。

▓ He's up to date with the U.S. market.　　他知道最新的美國市場消息。

▓ We have exactly *the right person* to assist you.　　我們恰好有適當的人選來協助您。

▓ I have just the person for you.　　我有適當人選給您。

▓ He knows more about this product than anyone here.　　他對這項產品，比這裏的任何人都知道得多。

▓ He has had a lot of experience *in this field*.　　在這方面，他有很多經驗。

▓ Our technical development department may be familiar with the problem.　　我們的技術開發部門，也許熟悉這個問題。

---

promotion〔prə'moʃən〕*n.*〔由宣傳〕促進銷售
development〔dɪ'vɛləpmənt〕*n.* 開發　　*up to date* 最新的
technical〔'tɛknɪkḷ〕*adj.* 技術上的

UNIT 3

Leading a tour of a factory
帶領參觀工廠

<對話精華>

· Please **feel free** to ask any questions.
有任何問題，請隨意發問。

· That's dangerous. **Please keep off.**
那很危險，請勿靠近。

· **We're running on three shifts.** 我們採三(輪)班制。

❊ 帶領訪客參觀工廠 ❊

▨ Now I'm going to take you to
our plant.

現在，我要帶您到我們的
工廠去。

▨ We'll **drive to** our plant, which
is about thirty minutes from
here.

我們將開車到工廠，從這
兒到工廠大約是三十分鐘
的車程。

▨ Let me show you **around** the plant.

讓我帶您看看工廠。

▨ I'll show you around.

我會帶您到處看看。

▨ A: Would you like to take a tour?

A：您要不要參觀一下呢?

B: **Lead** the way, please.

B：請帶路。

**

lead the way 帶路

※ 帶領參觀時常說的話 ※

▨ *This way, please.* 　　　　　　請這邊走。

▨ Please come with me. 　　　　請跟我來。

▨ Would you come this way, please? 　請這邊走好嗎？

▨ We're going up to the third floor. 　我們要上三樓去。

▨ We'll turn right there. 　　　　我們要在那邊右轉。

▨ That's dangerous. Please *keep off*. 　那很危險。請勿靠近。

▨ A: Where is the bathroom? 　　A：盥洗室在哪？

　 B: If you go straight down the hall, it's on your right. 　B：如果您沿走廊直走，就在您的右邊。

▨ You'll find it at the end of the hall. 　您會在走廊的盡頭找到它。

▨ It's right over there. 　　　　就在那邊。

※ 詢問訪客有無問題要提出 ※

▨ Please *feel free* to ask any questions. 　有任何問題，請隨意發問。

▨ Please feel free to ask me anything you want to know. 　您想知道什麼，請您隨意發問。

---

keep off 遠離　　hall〔hɔl〕*n.* 走廊

▓ Is there anything else you'd like to ask?　有什麼您想問的嗎？

❋ 無法回答問題時 ❋

▓ I'm sorry, but I'm not familiar with that (area).　很抱歉，我對那方面不熟悉。

▓ I'm sorry, but I don't know the answer, either.　很抱歉，我也不曉得答案。

▓ I'll *get* someone *who is familiar with that*.　我會找熟悉那方面的人來。

▓ Please talk to the production manager.　請與生產部經理談。

▓ Please ask him. He knows a lot about it.　請您問他。他對那個懂得很多。

▓ I'm sorry but that's *confidential*. I can't answer your question.　很抱歉，那是機密。我無法回答您的問題。

▓ I'm sorry but it hasn't been decided yet, so I can't say anything at this point.　很抱歉，那還沒決定，所以這點我無法談。

✳✳────────────────────

production〔prə'dʌkʃən〕*n.* 產品
confidential〔,kɑnfə'dɛnʃəl〕*adj.* 機密的

※ 各部門的工作 ※

■ What are those people doing over there? 　　那些人在那裏做什麼？

■ What's that office there?　　那邊那個是什麼辦公室？

■ What is that machine over there?　　那邊那部是什麼機器？

■ They are checking for quality.　　他們正在檢查品質。

■ The *assembly* is done here.　　裝配是在這裏進行。

■ Over here is one of the testing areas.　　這裏是測試區之一。

■ He's a test technician.　　他是個測試技術員。

■ Each piece is checked before it's used.　　每一件在使用前都經過檢查。

■ We check each component before we install it.　　每一部分在安裝前，我們都做過檢查。

■ The finished products come off the *conveyor* there.　　成品從那裏的輸送帶出來。

**──────────────

quality 〔'kwɑlətɪ〕 *n.* 品質　　assembly 〔ə'sɛmblɪ〕 *n.* 裝配
technician 〔tɛk'nɪʃən〕 *n.* 技術人員
component 〔kəm'ponənt〕 *n.* 部分　　conveyor 〔kən'veɚ〕 *n.* 輸送帶

✳ 關於產量 ✳

▨ What's your present production rate？　你們目前的生產率是多少？

▨ What's your annual production？　你們的年產量是多少？

▨ The **annual output** is about 150,000 units．　年產量約十五萬台。

▨ The **daily output** is 3,000 tons．　日產量是三千噸。

▨ In this plant, we produce about 20,000 units per month．　在這工廠，我們每月約生產兩萬台。

▨ Do you have any difficulty in meeting your production schedules？　在配合生產進度方面，你們有任何困難嗎？

✳ 關於生產力 ✳

▨ What's your productive capacity？　你們的生產力如何？

▨ This plant's productive capacity is 3,000 units a week．　這工廠的生產力是一星期三千台。

▨ We're operating at full capacity．　我們正全力生產。

---

annual〔'ænjʊəl〕 *adj.* 全年的　　output〔'aʊt,pʊt〕*n.* 產量
productive capacity 生產力　　operate〔'ɑpə,ret〕*v.* 運轉

▓ We are at about seventy percent capacity for one shift now. | 目前我們一個輪班，約有百分之七十的生產力。

▓ *We're running on three shifts.* | 我們採三（輪）班制。

❀ 關於品管 ❀

▓ How's your quality control? | 你們的品管如何？

▓ Our rejection rate is less than two percent. | 我們的退貨率，低於百分之二。

▓ How do your quality control systems operate? | 你們的品管系統是如何運作的？

▓ Is production ever slowed down because of any complaints by the quality control division? | 生產曾經因為品管部的不滿，而有減慢的情形嗎？

▓ How large is your repair and warranty section here at the plant? | 你們這工廠裏的修理和品質保證部門有多大？

▓ *We're very proud of* our quality control. | 我們頗以我們的品管為傲。

▓ We're quite proud of our quality control procedure. | 我們深以我們的品管程序為傲。

----

shift〔ʃɪft〕*n.* 輪值之一班
rejection〔rɪˈdʒɛkʃən〕*n.* 被拋棄或被拒絕之物
warranty〔ˈwɔrəntɪ〕*n.* 保證　　procedure〔prəˈsidʒɚ〕*n.* 程序

■ We always pay attention to improving our quality. 　　我們一直很注意改良品質。

■ We're always concerned with plant maintenance. 　　我們一直很關心工廠的維護。

✿ 關於技術開發 ✿

■ How big is the research department? 　　研究部門有多大？

■ Are you developing any new products? 　　你們有在發展什麼新產品嗎？

■ We have five laboratories. 　　我們有五間實驗室。

■ *We have a full-time staff of* twenty engineers. 　　我們有二十名的全職工程師。

■ What's your budget for R and D? 　　你們研究開發的預算是多少？

■ We spend over a million dollars on R and D each year. 　　我們每年花超過一百萬元在研究開發上。

■ Two percent of total sales is spent on R and D. 　　總銷售額的百分之二，是花費在研究開發上。

■ We're developing new model engines here. 　　我們這裏正在發展新型的引擎。

**

maintenance〔ˈmentənəns〕*n.* 維持；保養　　budget〔ˈbʌdʒɪt〕*n.* 預算
R and D：research and development

❋ 關於設備投資 ❋

▨ **We're equipped with** the latest equipment.

我們擁有最新的設備。

▨ We've spent a great deal of money on equipment.

我們在設備上已投下巨額的金錢。

▨ It's expensive, but it's better in the long run.

（設備）雖然貴，但就長遠看來是有利的。

▨ We're trying to **become more efficient**.

我們一直想要變得更有效率。

✱✱

in the long run 到後來；終久

efficient〔ɪˈfɪʃənt〕*adj.* 有效率的；最經濟的

UNIT 4

After a tour of a factory
參觀工廠後

＜對話精華＞

- How about a *coffee break*？ 休息一下，喝杯咖啡如何？
- How about lunch？ 一塊兒午餐如何？
- What did you think of our plant？
  您對於我們工廠有何看法？

＊ 提議休息和用餐 ＊

▓ Why don't we *take* a coffee break？	我們何不休息一下，喝杯咖啡？
▓ *How about a coffee break*？	休息一下，喝杯咖啡如何？
▓ Shall we take a break for a while？	我們暫時休息一下好嗎？
▓ Let's take a break for a while.	讓我們暫時休息一下。
▓ Say, it's about lunch time.	嘿，差不多到午餐時間了。
▓ It's almost time for lunch.	差不多是吃午餐的時候了。

coffee break 工作時之喝咖啡休息（通常在上午十時左右或下午三時前後）

■ Why don't the three of us go out to lunch?	我們三個人何不一塊出去午餐？
■ *How about lunch*?	一塊兒午餐如何？
■ Would you like to discuss it *over* lunch?	您願意一邊吃午餐，一邊討論嗎？
■ I'd like to discuss a few details over lunch.	我想一邊吃午餐，一邊討論幾項細節。

※ 談參觀工廠的感想 ※

■ *What did you think of our plant*?	您對於我們工廠有何看法？
■ Having seen our plant, what's your *overall impression*?	參觀過我們的工廠後，您整個的印象如何？
■ Very impressive.	令人印象深刻。
■ You certainly have a big operation.	你們經營的規模實在很大。
■ You have very fine facilities here.	你們這兒的設備相當好。
■ You have a very efficient plant.	你們是個很有效率的工廠。

** ─────────────────

detail〔'ditel〕*n.* 細節　　plant〔plænt〕*n.* 工廠
overall〔'ovɚ,ɔl〕*adj.* 全面的　　facilties〔fə'sɪlətɪz〕*n.(pl.)* 設備

詢問・徵信

基礎會話

CHAPTER III

UNIT 1

Inquiring about a company's business standing
詢問公司商譽

＜對話精華＞

- One of our business friends suggested that I call.
  一位我們生意上的友人，建議我打電話來。

- *May we ask the names of* your banks?
  能否請問貴公司往來銀行的名稱？

- Please ask Bank of Taiwan about our *business standing.* 有關我們公司的商譽，請向臺灣銀行查詢。

※ 表示對某家公司感興趣 ※

○ One of our business friends suggested that I call. 　　一位我們生意上的友人，建議我打電話來。

○ Johnson Company recommended your company. 　　強森公司推薦貴公司。

○ Your company has been recommended to me by the British Embassy in Hongkong. 　　香港的英國大使館向我推薦貴公司。

**

recommend〔͵rɛkə'mɛnd〕*v.* 推薦
embassy〔'ɛmbəsɪ〕*n.* 大使館

◑ The name of your company has been mentioned to me by *a business associate*.

貴公司的名字，是由一位商業夥伴向我提起的。

◑ This is a letter of introduction.

這是一封介紹信。

◑ I'm familiar with your name. I'd like to ask if we could *do business with* you.

我很熟悉您的姓名。我想問一問我們是否能與您做生意。

◑ I know your excellent products. We hope to *trade with* you.

我知道你們的產品優良。我們希望跟您做生意。

◑ I saw your advertisement in the Wall Street Journal.

我在華爾街日報上，看過你們的廣告。

◑ We saw your new product at the Los Angeles *Trade Fair*.

我們在洛杉磯商展中，看過你們的新產品。

◑ We're very interested in the product you exhibited at the international exhibition.

我們對你們在國際展覽會上展出的產品，極有興趣。

◑ We've studied your products very carefully.

我們曾詳細研究過你們的產品。

◑ Your products are almost exactly what we're looking for.

貴公司的產品，簡直就像是我們所要找的。

----

associate〔əˈsoʃɪɪt〕*n.* 夥伴   trade〔tred〕*v.* 交易
journal〔ˈdʒɝnḷ〕*n.* 日報；日記；雜誌   *trade fair* 商展
exhibition〔͵ɛksəˈbɪʃən〕*n.* 展覽會

✳ 詢問對方的經營狀況 ✳

◖ May we ask the names of your banks? 　能否請問貴公司往來銀行的名稱?

◖ Could you tell us which one is your main bank? 　您能告訴我們,你們主要的銀行是哪一家嗎?

◖ May we ask the names of your *references*? 　我們能請問你們保證人的姓名嗎?

◖ *For any information about our standing*, please contact the Bank of Taiwan in Taipei. 　如需有關我們信譽的資料,請和台北市的臺灣銀行連絡。

◖ Please ask Bank of Taiwan about our *business standing*. 　有關我們公司的營業狀況,請向臺灣銀行查詢。

◖ We'd like to see your annual report for the last three years. 　我們想看看貴公司過去三年來的年度報告。

◖ Here's the financial report of our company. 　這裏是本公司的財務報告。

◖ These are the profit and loss figures. 　這些是損益數目。

✳✳────────────────────

reference〔'rɛfərəns〕*n.* 保證人;參考人;證明書
standing〔'stændɪŋ〕*n.* 地位;名望
figures〔'fɪgjəz, 'fɪgəz〕*n. pl.* 數字

UNIT 2

Credit investigation
信用調查

> **＜對話精華＞**
>
> ・How is their credit? 他們的信用如何？
> ・*There is no record of* a loan ever being refused.
> 　不曾有被拒絕貸款的記錄。
> ・They're *deeply in debt*. 他們負債累累。

● Please let us know about the credibility of Scott and Cooper Company.

請告訴我們史考特暨古柏公司的信用狀況。

● Do you know anything about the financial standing of this company?

您知道有關這家公司的財務狀況嗎？

● *How is their credit*?

他們的信用如何？

● The Bank of America grants them unsecured letters of credit.

美國銀行授與他們無擔保信用狀。

＊＊────────────────

credibility〔͵krɛdə'bɪlətɪ〕*n.* 可信性；可靠性
grant〔grænt〕*v.* 批准；授與
unsecured〔͵ʌnsɪ'kjʊrd〕*adj.* 沒有抵押的；沒有擔保的

◑ There is no record of a loan ever being refused.　　不曾有被拒絕貸款的記錄。

◑ There has been no recent need for long-term or short-term *borrowing*.　　最近無需長期或短期的貸款。

◑ How about their latest sales figures?　　他們最近的銷售額如何？

◑ Their sales have actually gone down.　　實際上，他們的銷售額已經走下坡了。

◑ They're *deeply in debt*.　　他們負債累累。

◑ I suggest you not trade with this company.　　我建議您不要與這家公司交易。

◑ This company is very *promising*.　　這家公司的前途看好。

◑ They're well-established and reliable.　　他們的地位穩固又可靠。

◑ How is this company capitalized?　　這家公司是如何設定資本的?

◑ How's their experience?　　他們的經驗如何？

**———————————

in debt 欠債　　promising〔ˊprɑmɪsɪŋ〕*adj.* 有前途的
well-established 已為大眾接受的；已建立地位的
capitalize〔ˊkæpətḷ͵aɪz〕*v.* 定（某公司之）資本額

◖ They haven't had much experience in importing.

他們進口方面的經驗不很豐富。

◖ They've had a little experience importing from a Japanese company.

他們作日本方面的進口，有一點經驗。

◖ *They're already distributing* electrical products for a Japanese company.

他們已經在爲一家日本公司，經銷電器產品了。

✽✽————————————

distribute〔dɪˈstrɪbjʊt〕v. 經銷；分配

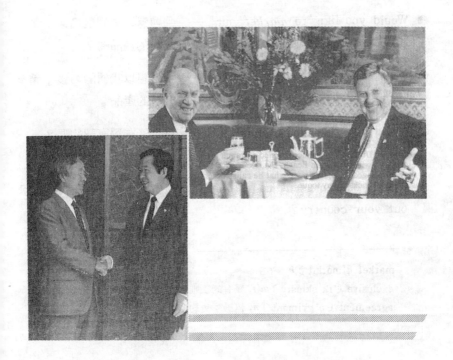

UNIT 3

Inquiring about the other party's interest for business
詢問對方交易的意願

＜對話精華＞

· Would you like to *market* our products under your name? 您願意以您們的名義，銷售我們的產品嗎？

· Would you like an *exclusive* agreement？
  您希望有獨賣契約嗎？

◑ Would you like to *market* our products under your name？ | 您願意以你們的名義，銷售我們的產品嗎？

◑ We'd like to sell your products under our name. | 我們想以我們的名義，銷售您們的產品。

◑ Would you like an *exclusive* agreement？ | 您希望有獨賣契約嗎？

◑ Would you represent us throughout your country？ | 請您們在貴國各地代表本公司好嗎？

**

market〔'mɑrkɪt〕*v.* 銷售
exclusive〔ɪk'sklusɪv〕*adj.* 獨有的；唯一的
agreement〔ə'grimənt〕*n.* 協議；契約

UNIT 4

About the agent
關於代理商

<對話精華>

- Will you consider our proposal to **act as** your agent?
  您能考慮我們的提議，做你們的代理商嗎？
- We have an **exclusive** agent in this area already.
  這地區我們已經有獨家代理商了。

※ 找尋代理商 ※

❶ We'd like to sell our products in the United States.

我們想在美國，銷售我們的產品。

❶ We're looking for an agent to **handle** our products.

我們正在尋找代理商，來經銷我們的產品。

❶ **We're interested in** locating an exclusive agent to sell our electrical appliances.

我們有意找一個獨家代理商，來經銷本公司的電氣製品。

❶ We're looking for a suitable a-gent to represent us in Taipei.

我們正在台北尋找合適的代理商，來代表本公司。

**——

agent〔'edʒənt〕n. 代理商   handle〔'hændl〕v. 經銷
appliance〔ə'plaɪəns〕n. 用具；電器用品

◗ Are you interested in representing us in the United States?　您有興趣在美國代表本公司嗎？

◗ We'd like you to be our agent if you're at all interested.　如果您極有興趣的話，我們想要您當我們的代理商。

✳ 想擔任代理商 ✳

◗ We're interested in acting as your *sole distributor*.　我們有意思做你們獨家的經銷商。

◗ We'd like to sell your products.　我們想銷售貴公司的產品。

◗ We're willing to sell your products.　我們願意銷售貴公司的產品。

◗ Will you consider our proposal to *act as* your agent?　您能考慮我們的提議，做您們的代理商嗎？

◗ If prices and other conditions are right, we're ready to become your agent.　如果價錢和其他條件適合的話，我們準備成爲貴公司的代理商。

✳ 拒絕新代理商的申請 ✳

◗ We have an *exclusive agent* in this area already.　這地區我們已經有獨家代理商了。

------

proposal〔prə'pozl〕*n*. 提議

◑ We're not in a position to
 take on any further agents.

我們不能夠再多雇用代理商。

◑ We don't need a new agent at
 this stage.

我們現階段,還不需要新的代
理商。

◑ We have a large number of
 agents in the United States
 already.

我們在美國已經有很多代理商
了。

◑ We have not made any decision about an agency yet.

我們還沒決定要用代理商。

**————————————

 take on 採用;雇用   stage〔stedʒ〕*n.* 階段

UNIT 5

About the offer
關於報價

<對話精華>

· What did you think about that offer?
  您認為那個報價如何?

· We may make a *counteroffer*. 我們可以還價。

· Could you *make* a more favorable offer?
  您能出個更合適的價錢嗎?

○ I hope this offer will be suitable to you. | 我希望這個報價會適合您。

○ What did you think about that offer? | 您認為那個報價如何?

○ *We may make a counteroffer*. | 我們可以還價。

○ Could you make a more favorable offer? | 您能出個更合適的價錢嗎?

○ I'm sorry but we've decided not to accept your offer. | 很抱歉,我們已經決定不接受你們的報價。

○ We'll accept your offer. | 我們將接受您的報價。

**

offer〔'ɔfɚ〕*n.* 報價;提議
counteroffer〔'kaʊntɚˌɔfɚ〕*n.* 反報價;還價

談論公司
基礎會話

CHAPTER
IV

UNIT 1

Talking about the office
談論公司

<對話精華>

· ***Have you heard of*** our company before?
  您以前曾聽過本公司嗎?

· I got the name of your company from a friend.
  貴公司的名字,我是從一位朋友那兒知道的。

◑ ***Have you heard of*** our company before?　您以前曾聽過本公司嗎?

◑ ***Do you happen to know*** our company?　您知道本公司嗎?

◑ Perhaps you're acquainted with our firm.　或許您知道本公司。

◑ I hear about your company often.　我常聽說貴公司。

◑ I've read about your firm in newspapers and magazines.　我曾在報章雜誌上,讀過有關貴公司的消息。

◑ Your company is well known in Taiwan.　貴公司在台灣相當有名。

◑ I got the name of your company from a friend.　貴公司的名字,我是從一位朋友那兒知道的。

UNIT 2

Company history & organization
公司的歷史及規模組織

＜對話精華＞

- When *was* your company *founded*?
  貴公司何時創立的？
- Let me *explain a little* about our company.
  讓我簡單說明一下本公司。
- We have five plants *in various parts of* Taiwan.
  我們有五家工廠，分散在台灣各地。

❋ 談公司的歷史 ❋

◐ When was your company founded?　　貴公司何時創立的？

◐ Our company was established in
　1952.　　本公司創立於一九五二年。

◐ Our company was founded seventy
　years ago.　　本公司創立於七十年前。

◐ We're a *young* company, only about
　ten years old.　　我們是新興的公司，才只
　有大約十年的歷史。

**

　young〔jʌŋ〕*adj.* 新建立的；新興的

◑ Our company will soon have its eightieth anniversary.　本公司就快要創業八十周年了。

◑ Let me explain a little about our company.　讓我簡單說明一下本公司。

◑ Our paper manufacturing company is the oldest in Taiwan.　我們是全臺灣最老的一家造紙公司。

◑ We've been in business for thirty years.　我們已經經商三十年了。

◑ Our company *was founded* ten years ago as an *affiliate* of Hung-kuan Trading Company.　本公司創立於十年前，是宏冠貿易公司的關係企業。

◑ Fifteen years ago two banks merged to form this bank.　十五年前，兩家銀行合併成現在這家銀行。

◑ Initially, we designed and made medical instruments.　起初，我們設計並製造醫療器材。

◑ Ten years ago we went into the pharmaceutical field.　十年前，我們進入製藥界。

----

anniversary 〔͵ænə'vɝsərɪ〕 *n.* 周年；周年紀念　　*in business* 經商
affiliate 〔ə'fɪlɪ͵et〕 *n.* 支會；主權之一部或全部屬於另一公司之商業機構
merge 〔mɝdʒ〕 *v.* 合併；兼併
pharmaceutical 〔͵fɑrmə'sjutɪkl̩〕 *adj.* 製藥的

❋ 公司的規模和組織 ❋

● Our company is the largest printer in Taiwan.　　本公司是臺灣最大的印刷公司。

● Our company is the third largest auto company in Taiwan.　　本公司是臺灣第三大汽車公司。

● Our company is one of the major food makers.　　本公司是主要食品製造商之一。

● How many employees do you have?　　你們有多少員工？

● Two hundred in the office and 500 in the plant.　　辦公室有兩百名，工廠有五百名。

● We have about 2,000 employees.　　我們大約有二千名員工。

● We have over 20,000 employees *including* those working in the affiliated company.　　包括分公司在內，我們有超過兩萬名的員工。

● Where is your *head office*?　　你們的總公司在哪？

● Where is your main plant?　　你們的主廠在哪？

● We have five plants *in various parts of* Taiwan.　　我們有五家工廠，分散在台灣各地。

❋❋

employee〔͵ɛmplɔɪ'i〕*n.* 員工

UNIT 3

公司經營的範圍、
市場及銷售體制

╔══════════════════════════════════╗

＜對話精華＞

· What sort of products *do you deal with*?
　你們作哪方面產品的買賣？

· We *handle* medical instruments primarily.
　　我們主要是經銷醫療設備。

· *We're importers of* kitchen appliances.
　　我們是廚房用具進口商。

╚══════════════════════════════════╝

❈ 公司的經營範圍 ❈

◑ What *line* of business are you
　in?

你們從事哪方面的行業？

◑ What are your main products?

你們主要生產什麼？

◑ What sort of products do you
　import?

你們進口哪方面的產品？

◑ What sort of products do you
　deal with?

你們作哪方面產品的買賣？

**────────────────────

　　line〔laɪn〕*n.* 行業；本行
　　deal〔dil〕*v.* 交易；經營；買賣（與 with 或 in 連用）

◑ We deal in office equipment. 　　　我們作辦公室設備的買賣。

◑ We sell electrical appliances 　　　我們主要是銷售電氣製品。
primarily.

◑ We **handle** medical instruments 　　我們主要是經銷醫療設備。
primarily.

◑ *We supply a wide range of* 　　　我們提供多種不同的辦公室
office automation devices. 　　　　自動化設備。

◑ We manufacture printing ma- 　　　我們製造印刷機和影印機。
chines and copying machines.

◑ We make **sound** systems such 　　　我們製造如錄音機和立體音
as tape recorders and stereo 　　　響之類的有聲系統。
sets.

◑ We produce *a wide variety of* 　　　我們生產一般大衆所使用的
electronic equipment used by 　　　各種電子設備。
the general public.

◑ We're a manufacturer and sell- 　　　我們是高級服飾的製造商兼
er of quality fabrics. 　　　　　售賣商。

◑ We're importers of kitchen 　　　　我們是厨房用具進口商。
appliances.

** ————————————————————

primarily 〔'praɪ,mɛrəlɪ 〕*adv.* 主要地
automation 〔,ɔtə'meʃən〕*n.* 自動化機器　　*tape recorder* 錄音機
electronic 〔ɪ,lɛk'trɑnɪk 〕*adj.* 電子的

● We're developing software for computers. 　　我們正在發展電腦用的軟體。

● We provide many components for well-known companies. 　　我們提供很多零件給知名的公司。

❋ 市場與銷售地區 ❋

● Who is your biggest market? 　　你們最大的市場是誰？

● Do you export your products to Asia too? 　　你們也將產品輸出到亞洲嗎？

● Is the U.S. your largest market? 　　美國是你們最大的市場嗎？

● How many **branch offices** do you have? 　　你們有多少分公司？

● Do you have a branch office on the West Coast? 　　你們在西海岸有分公司嗎？

● How many territories do you have? 　　你們有多少銷售地區？

● Our main activity is in the States. 　　我們主要的活動範圍是在美國。

** ─────────────

software〔'sɔft,wer〕*n.* 軟體
component〔kəm'ponənt〕*n.* 成份
branch office 分公司

● We *cover* the U.S. west of the Mississippi. 　　　我們銷售地區包括美國密西西比河西部。

● Our trade with Southeast Asia is growing. 　　　我們對東南亞的貿易正在成長。

● We do business in thirty countries. 　　　我們在三十個國家中都有貿易。

● We have over thirty branches abroad. 　　　我們在海外有三十家以上的分公司。

● We have offices in every major country. 　　　在每個主要國家，我們都有分公司。

● We've recently opened a branch in Bangkok. 　　　我們最近在曼谷開了一家分公司。

※ 銷售體制 ※

● Could you tell me about your *sales network*? 　　　能不能跟我談談你們的銷售網？

● What are your major channels of distribution? 　　　你們主要的銷售管道是什麼？

● How many service centers do you have? 　　　你們有多少服務中心？

***

sales network 銷售網　　channel〔ˊtʃænl〕*n.* 途徑；管道
service center 服務中心

◑ How many repair shops do you have? 你們有多少修理廠?

◑ How many people do you have in sales? 你們銷售方面的人員有多少?

◑ We have a total of fifty-five sales agents. 我們總共有五十五家銷售代理商。

◑ We have sales and service centers in most major industrial areas. 大多數的主要工業區,我們都有銷售和服務中心。

◑ We're proud of our sales force. 我們以我們的銷售力爲傲。

❉ 銷售量及市場佔有率 ❉

◑ What's the total amount of your annual sales? 你們每年的總銷售量是多少?

◑ It's about $300,000,000. 大約是三億美元。

◑ Our *turnover* last year was $650,000,000. 我們去年的總營業額是六億五千萬美元。

◑ How about the latest sales figures? 最近銷售額如何呢?

---

sales 〔selz〕 *n. pl.* 銷售工作; 售貨總量
turnover 〔'tɜn,ovɚ〕 *n.* 某一時期的總營業額

◑ How were your sales last year? | 你們去年銷路如何?

◑ Our sales were up twelve percent last year. | 我們去年的銷售量,提升了十二個百分點。

◑ What's your *market share*? | 你們的市場佔有率是多少?

◑ It's about fifteen percent. | 大約是十五個百分點。

◑ We have a thirty-five percent market share. | 我們有三十五個百分點的市場佔有率。

◑ We have about thirty percent of the market in compact cars. | 我們的小型車,大約佔有百分之三十的市場。

◑ *Our brand of* beer has a sixty percent share of the market. | 我們這種品牌的啤酒,佔了百分之六十的市場。

◑ It seems you've done quite well. | 看來您似乎做得不錯。

** ————————————

sale〔sel〕*n.* 銷路　　*market share* 市場佔有率

———— 學英文的書,學習都有 ————

UNIT 4

Talking about office procedure
談論公司的制度

＊ <對話精華> ＊

· Our union *rarely goes on strike*. 我們的工會很少罷工。

· What *fringe benefits* do you offer your employees?
你們提供員工什麼樣的福利呢？

· The company provides housing *at a nominal charge*.
公司是以象徵性的收費提供住宿。

＊ 業務員的給薪制度 ＊

◑ May I ask how your salesmen are compensated?

可否請問你們的售貨員如何給薪？

◑ Could you tell me how you pay them?

可否請你告訴我，你們怎麼付他們薪水的？

◑ How is your salesmen's compensation plan set up?

你們售貨員給薪制度是如何建立的？

◑ It's a *basic salary* plus *commission*.

底薪加上酬勞獎金。

＊＊

compensate〔'kɑmpən,set〕*v*. 報酬
commission〔kə'mɪʃən〕*n*. 佣金；酬勞金

◑ Their income is based on sales activity.

他們的收入是根據銷售成績。

◑ Aside from the commission, there is a *substantial bonus*.

除了酬勞金之外，還有豐富的紅利。

※ 勞資關係及勞動狀況 ※

◑ Does your company have a *labor union*?

你們公司有沒有勞工聯盟？

◑ Is your labor union very strong?

你們的勞工聯盟勢力大不大？

◑ We have excellent relations with our employees.

我們和員工之間的關係良好。

◑ Both labor and management recognize that job security is very important.

勞工和管理階層都認為，工作的安全保障很重要。

◑ Our union *rarely goes on strike*.

我們的工會很少罷工。

◑ Our products would never be delayed because of a strike.

我們的產品，絕不會因罷工而延遲交貨。

◑ What are the *office hours* in your company?

你們公司的辦公時間呢？

**

activity〔æk'tɪvətɪ〕*n*. 活動力；積極性
substantial〔səb'stænʃəl〕*adj*. 實質上的；豐富的；很多的
bonus〔'bonəs〕*n*. 紅利；特別津貼　　strike〔straɪk〕*n*. 罷工

◑ Our office hours are from nine until five.　　我們的辦公時間從九點到五點。

◑ Our company works a forty-hour week.　　本公司一星期工作四十個鐘頭。

◑ We have a five-day work week in our company.　　本公司一星期工作五天。

◑ We work *every other* Saturday until three.　　我們每隔一周的禮拜六，必須工作到三點。

◑ Do you have much overtime?　　你們要常加班嗎？

◑ We often *work overtime*.　　我們經常加班。

◑ We don't work overtime very often.　　我們不常加班。

❋ 福利設施 ❋

◑ Do you provide *recreation facilities* for your employees?　　你們有提供娛樂設施給你們的員工嗎？

◑ We have recreation facilities for our employees.　　我們有員工娛樂設施。

◑ Our plant has a playground and a gym.　　我們工廠有運動場和體育館。

**

overtime〔'ovə,taɪm〕*n.* 加班時間；超出定時的時間

recreation〔,rɛkrɪ'eʃən〕*n.* 娛樂　　gym〔dʒɪm〕*n.* 〔俗〕體育館

● We have a clinic in our company. 　我們公司裏有一個診所。

● These facilities are open for all
　our employees. 　這些設施是開放給所有員工的。

● These facilities are *free* for
　our employees. 　這些設施是免費提供給我們員工的。

● What *fringe benefits* do you of-
　fer your employees? 　你們提供員工什麼樣的福利呢？

● The company provides housing
　at a nominal charge. 　公司是以象徵性的收費，提供住宿。

● Lunch is provided at cost in
　the cafeteria. 　餐廳裏提供非常便宜的午餐。

**——————————————————

clinic 〔'klınık〕 *n.* 診所　　　*fringe benefit* 固定薪金以外之福利
nominal 〔'namənļ〕 *adj.* 象徵性的
cost 〔kɔst〕 *n.* 費用；損失；犧牲（*at cost* 表示以犧牲價來賣，引申為
　　「非常便宜」的意思）

UNIT 5

Miscellaneous
其 他

＜對話精華＞

· We do a *direct mail* campaign once a year.
  我們一年做一次直接寄送的活動。

· *TV commercials* are an effective means of advertising. 電視商業廣告是很有效的廣告方法。

· Do you have much competition in the United States?
  你們在美國的競爭激烈嗎？

※ 所利用的宣傳媒體 ※

◑ What kind of advertising have you been using for your goods?

你們的產品，一直是作什麼樣的廣告？

◑ We're constantly putting *ads* in newspapers, popular magazines and in trade journals.

我們不斷地在報紙、暢銷雜誌及貿易雜誌上登廣告。

◑ We advertise in newspapers and popular magazines.

我們在報紙及暢銷雜誌上登廣告。

---

advertising〔'ædvɚ͵taɪzɪŋ〕*n.* 廣告；廣告業

◑ We *do a direct mail* campaign once a year.　　　　　　　　我們一年做一次直接寄送的活動。

◑ We're thinking of advertising on TV.　　　　　　　　　我們一直想在電視上打廣告。

◑ *TV commercials* are an effective means of advertising.　　　　　　電視商業廣告是很有效的廣告方法。

◑ We *consult with* a manufacturer to decide what is the best way to advertise.　　　　　　我們和製造業者商量，以決定哪一種廣告方式最好。

◑ How much do you spend on advertising each year?　　　　你們每年花多少廣告費？

◑ What's your budget for advertising?　　　　　　　　你們廣告的預算是多少？

❋ 關於競爭的公司 ❋

◑ *Do you have much competition* in the United States?　　　　你們在美國的競爭激烈嗎？

◑ Who are your main competitors?　　　　　　　誰是你們最主要的競爭對象?

◑ We have several competitors in Taiwan.　　　　　　　我們在台灣有許多競爭對手。

---

campaign〔kæm'pen〕*n.* 活動（為某種目的而活動）
commercial〔kə'mɝʃəl〕*n.* 無線電或電視的商業廣告
manufacturer〔,mænjə'fæktʃərə〕*n.* 製造業者

Vocabulary Street 公司專用術語

- limited company 有限公司 (= *Ltd.*)
- unlimited company 無限公司　　affiliated company 聯營公司
- subsidiary company 附屬公司
- multinational corporation 多國公司
- transnational corporation 跨國公司 (= *internation corporation*)
- affiliated enterprise 關係企業

~~~~~~

- distributor 〔dɪ'strɪbjətɚ〕*n.* 中盤商 (=*middleman*)
- wholesale merchant 批發商
- general agent 總代理　　sole agent 獨家代理
- guild 〔gɪld〕*n.* 同業公會
- cooperative association 合作社
- smuggling ring 走私集團
- black market 黑市

~~~~~~

- silent partner 不出面合夥人
- a regular customer 老主顧 (= *old customer*)
- sell on consignment 代銷
- sales volume 銷售量
- circulation 〔,sɚkjə'leʃən〕*n.* 銷路

產品説明
基礎會話

CHAPTER
V

UNIT 1

Talking about seeing the products
談參觀產品

＜對話精華＞

· **Anything particular** that you're interested in?
有沒有您特別感興趣的？

· Our new product will soon **be on the market**.
我們的新產品，很快就要上市了。

· Recently we've developed better technology.
最近我們已發展出更優良的技術。

❈ 參觀產品 ❈

♤ We're interested in your products.　　　我們對你們的產品有興趣。

♠ We're very much interested in your personal computers.　　　我們對你們的個人電腦極感興趣。

♤ Please show me some samples.　　　請讓我看一些樣品。

♤ I'd like to show you our products.　　　我想讓您看看我們的產品。

---

product〔′prɑdʌkt〕*n.* 產物；生產品

♤ I'd like you to see our show-room. 　　　　我想讓您看看我們的（貨品）陳列室。

♤ Please look at our display products. 　　　　請看看我們的展示品。

♤ *Anything particular* that you're interested in? 　　　　有沒有您特別感興趣的？

♤ What would you like to see most? 　　　　您最想看什麼？

♤ Would you look at this product? 　　　　您要不要看看這個產品？

❋ 介紹新產品 ❋

♤ Please show me your new product. 　　　　請讓我看看你們的新產品。

♤ Do you have a *prototype* of your new product? 　　　　有沒有你們新產品的原型？

♤ When is this product going to *be on the market*? 　　　　這項產品何時上市？

♤ Our new model car will be out next month. 　　　　我們的新型車將在下個月上市。

·

showroom〔ʼʃo,rum, -,rʊm〕*n*. 貨品陳列室
display〔dɪʼsple〕*adj*. 作樣品陳列的；陳列的
prototype〔ʼprotə,taɪp〕*n*. 原型

♤ Our new product will soon be on the market.

我們的新產品，很快就要上市了。

♤ We've now developed a new product.

我們現在已發展出一種新產品。

♤ Recently we've developed better technology.

最近我們已發展出更優良的技術。

♤ This is our latest product.

這是我們最新的產品。

♤ This is our newest product.

這是我們最新的產品。

＊＊────────────

develop〔dɪ'vɛləp〕v. 發展　　technology〔tɛk'nɑlədʒɪ〕n. 技術

UNIT 2

Offering reference material on products
提供產品的參考資料

＜對話精華＞

- This is our *latest* catalog. 這是我們最新的目錄。
- Could I have this sample *free of charge*? 我能免費要這個樣品嗎？
- ... but we'll make a sample discount of twenty percent. …，不過，我們可以打八折當樣品。

❋ 提供說明書及目錄 ❋

♤ Shall I show you our product information sheet?	要不要看看我們的產品說明書？
♤ This is our *latest catalog*.	這是我們最新的目錄。
♤ Here is the catalog you asked for.	這是您要的目錄。
♤ This catalog shows most of our products.	這份目錄列有我們大部份產品。
♤ We have a pamphlet in English.	我們有一本英文（版）的小册子。

**

pamphlet〔'pæmflɪt〕*n.* 小册子

♤ Let me send you our catalog. 讓我寄我們的目錄給您。

♤ Do you have any printed material on this product? 你們有沒有這項產品的說明書？

♤ *Is there a catalog for* tape recorders? 有沒有錄音機的目錄？

✳ 提供樣品 ✳

♤ Shall I send you a sample later? 要不要我日後再寄個樣品給您？

♤ We'll send more to your office, *if you like*. 如果您喜歡的話，我們會多寄一些到貴公司。

♤ Please take this as a sample. 請拿這個當做樣品吧。

♤ Would it be possible for me to take a sample back with me? 我可以帶一個樣品回去嗎？

♤ Could I have this sample *free of charge*? 我能免費要這個樣品嗎？

♤ I'm sorry we can't give this as a sample but we'll *make a sample discount of* twenty percent. 很抱歉，這個我們不能當樣品給，不過，我們可以打八折當樣品。

---

tape recorder 錄音機　　discount〔ˈdɪskaʊnt〕*n.* 折扣

♤ Please send your brochure and a sample to our head office here.

請把你們的小冊子及樣品，寄到我們這裏的總公司來。

♤ Please send a sample immediately.

請立刻送一份樣品來。

♤ We'll order after we see the sample.

看過樣品後，我們會訂購。

＊＊─────────────

brochure〔bro'ʃur〕*n.* 小冊子

UNIT 3

About the circulation
關於銷路

<對話精華>

· There's been a **big rush** for it lately.
　這個最近造成大搶購。

· **There's a great demand** for our new product.
　我們的新產品需求量很大。

· In Taiwan, **it's selling like hot cakes**.
　在台灣，這很暢銷。

♠ How is the product selling?　　　産品賣得如何？

♠ It's selling well.　　　　　　　賣得很好。

♠ It's selling poorly.　　　　　　賣得很差。

♠ There's a great demand for
our new product.　　　　　　　我們的新産品需求量很大。

♠ There's been **a big rush** for it
lately.　　　　　　　　　　　這個最近造成大搶購。

♠ The goods are very much **in demand**. （這些）貨品的需求量很大。

** ────────────────

demand〔dɪˈmænd〕n. 需求　　　rush〔rʌʃ〕n. 搶購

♤ There is little demand for the goods. （這些）貨品的需求量不高。

♤ It has sold well here in Taiwan. 這個在台灣這裏賣得很好。

♤ In Taiwan, *it's selling like hot cakes*. 在台灣，這很暢銷。

♤ It's just come out, so we don't know the outcome yet. 才剛出品，因此我們還不知道結果。

♤ Which brand sells better? 那一種牌子賣得比較好？

♤ The DC-200 is the best-selling product of its kind. DC-200是同類產品中最暢銷的。

♤ How many sets do you sell a month? 你們一個月賣幾套？

♤ We sell more than 3,000 sets a month. 我們一個月賣三千套以上。

♤ We sold 255 sets last month. 上個月我們賣了兩百五十五套。

♤ This type of machine is in great demand. 這型的機器需求量很大。

♤ There's a growing demand for it. 這個的需求量正在增加。

**────────────

sell (or go) like hot cakes 〔俗〕現蒸熱賣；很好賣；暢銷

set 〔sɛt〕*n.* 組；套

♠ Is the demand for this product increasing?

這項產品的需求有沒有增加?

♠ There is no more demand for this product.

這項產品已不再有需求。

♠ Do you think there will be more demand for this product?

您想(這產品)還會不會有更多的需求?

♠ Good *publicity* will help this product sell better.

好的宣傳,會使這項產品賣得更好。

---

increasing〔ɪnˈkrisɪŋ〕*adj*. 日益增多的
publicity〔pʌbˈlɪsətɪ〕*n*. 廣告;宣傳

UNIT 4

Talking about a product's merits & benefits
談產品的優點及利益

<對話精華>

- The system we have adopted is *original*.
  我們所採用的系統是全新的。
- This car *gets good mileage*. 這輛車燃料很省。
- The equipment will *pay for itself* in two years.
  這項設備，兩年內便可收回成本。

※ 產品的優點 ※

♤ How is your product better than the competition?

你們的產品，哪裏優於其他競爭者？

♤ What are the selling points of your product?

你們銷售產品的要訣是什麼？

♤ Our product is over and above our rival's products and yet, we're able to sell it at the same price.

我們的產品超於競爭對手的產品之上，不過，我們可以以同樣的價格銷售。

**

competition 〔͵kɑmpə'tɪʃən〕 n. 競爭；角逐；競爭者
rival 〔'raɪvḷ〕 n. 對手；競爭者

♤ We can offer a superior product at the same price as our competitors' products in the same class.

同樣的東西，我們可以提供和我們競爭對手價格相同，但却是更高品質的產品。

♤ You will be able to *price* our products competitively in the United States.

您能夠幫我們的產品，訂一個在美國經得起競爭的價格。

♤ Compared with competing products, ours is smaller and lighter.

與競爭的產品比起來，我們的產品比較小，比較輕。

♤ Students and children like this computer because it's easy to operate.

學生和小孩喜歡這種電腦，因為它容易操作。

♤ Our products are easier to operate than our competitors'.

我們的產品，比競爭者的產品，容易操作。

♤ We take less time for an installation than our competition.

我們裝設所需的時間，比競爭對手少。

♤ The system we have adopted is original.

我們所採用的系統是全新的。

♤ This is the most powerful engine in its class.

在同類產品中，這是最有力的引擎。

---

price〔praɪs〕*v.* 估…之價　　installation〔ˌɪnstəˈleʃən〕*n.* 裝設
original〔əˈrɪdʒənḷ〕*adj.* 最初的；新的

♤ *This car gets good mileage*. 這輛車燃料很省。

♤ It's designed to *conserve* energy. 這種設計，是為了節省能源。

♤ One of the excellent points about this machine is that *it rarely needs servicing*. 這種機器最棒的優點之一，是很少需要維護。

♤ Our equipment can be repaired very quickly. 我們的設備，很快就可以修得好。

❋ 產品的利盆 ❋

♤ You can save ten percent of your energy costs by using this machine. 使用這種機器，您可以節省百分之十的燃料費。

♤ If you use this machine, your productivity will increase *by* twenty percent. 如果你們使用這種機器，你們的生產量，將可增加兩成。

♤ If the equipment can work three shifts per day, it can easily pay for itself in a year. 如果這種設備，一天三班都可以用，一年之內，便很容易就值回成本了。

♤ The equipment will *pay for itself* in two years. 這項設備，兩年內便可收回成本。

✻✻

mileage 〔'maɪlɪdʒ〕 *n.* 哩程　　conserve 〔kən'sɜv〕 *v.* 保存；保全

UNIT 5

Marketing a product
銷售產品

<對話精華>

· Our products are **well thought of** in Taiwan.
我們的產品在台灣有很好的評價。

· We **guarantee** its quality. 它的品質,我們可以保證。

· We **handle** only the best brands.
我們只經銷好牌子的東西。

♤ We make good equipment. 　　　　我們做的是很好的設備。

♤ Our products are **well thought of** in Taiwan. 　　　　我們的產品在台灣有很好的評價。

♤ We're confident about the quality of our products. 　　　　對於產品的品質,我們很有信心。

♤ We always do our best. 　　　　我們總是盡力求得最好。

♤ We **guarantee** its quality. 　　　　它的品質,我們可以保證。

♤ Our products are all quality goods. 　　　　我們的產品,全都是很有品質的。

·

equipment〔ɪ'kwɪpmənt〕*n.* 設備　　　guarantee〔͵gærən'ti〕*v.* 保證

♤ We *handle* only the best brands.   我們只經銷好牌子的東西。

♤ This brand is well-known.   這個牌子大家都知道。

♤ We *highly* recommend this product.   我們鄭重推薦這項產品。

♤ We *strongly* recommend this product.   我們極力推薦這項產品。

♤ I'm sure you'll be pleased with this.   我確信您對於這個，會很滿意的。

**

brand〔brænd〕*n*. 種類，牌子

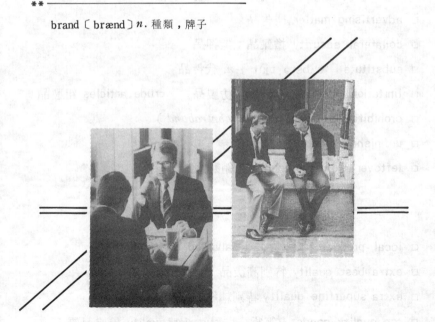

Vocabulary Street 樣品・產品專用術語

- original sample 原樣品　　duplicate sample 複樣品
- quality sample 品質樣品　　color sample 彩色樣品
- seller's sample 賣方樣品　　buyer's sample 買方樣品
- advance sample 先發樣品　　counter sample 對等樣品

- staple item 主要商品
- novelty〔ˋnɑvḷtɪ〕*n.* 新出品；最新製品
- advertising matter 廣告品
- collateral security 擔保品；抵押品
- substitute〔ˋsʌbstəˌtjut〕*n.* 代替品
- imitation〔ˌɪməˋteʃən〕*n.* 仿製品　　crude articles 粗製品
- prohibited goods 違禁品（＝*contraband*）
- unfinished product 半成品
- leftover export products 外銷剩餘品

- local products 本地貨　　salvaged goods 水漬貨
- extra best quality 特別高級品
- extra superfine quality 特別精細品
- top quality goods 上等貨　　superior quality 優良品質
- ordinary quality 中等品質　　inferior quality 劣等品質

議價・付款・售後服務
基礎會話

CHAPTER
VI

UNIT 1

Aspects of negotiating prices
議價之種種狀況

＜對話精華＞

- Please *quote* us a price for the machine.
  這部機器，請給我們開個價。

- *Are all the quotations C.I.F.?*
  所有的報價，都以C.I.F. 來算嗎？

- Could you give us *more of a discount*?
  您能不能多給我們一點折扣？

❋ 詢問價格 ❋

♤ Please send the catalog and price list.　　　　　請寄目錄和價目表來。

♤ How much is this?　　　　　這個多少錢？

♤ What is the price?　　　　　價錢是多少？

♤ Please *quote* us a price for the machine.　　　　　這部機器，請給我們開個價。

♤ The price depends on quantity.　　　　　價格要依數量而定。

**

quote〔kwot〕*v*. 開價；報價　　quantity〔'kwɑntətɪ〕*n*. 數量；大量

♤ I can't say **offhand** exactly how much.

我不能立刻決定確實是多少錢。

♤ The price is $1.50 per yard.

價格是每碼美金一塊五。

♤ The list price is $250 per unit.

目錄標價是每台兩百五十美元。

♤ We can give them to you for $185.50 per unit.

我們可以賣您們，每台美金一百八十五元五角。

♤ The price is $200 per ton.

價格是每噸二百美元。

♤ You mean per short ton?

您是指每一美噸？

♤ Is the weight the same as it was **on arrival**?

送達時，重量是不是一樣呢？

♤ We price the weight at the time of shipment.

我們在裝船時，依重量訂價。

♤ What about the loss in weight during transportation?

運送中，損失的重量怎麼辦？

♤ We will compensate for any loss in weight over two percent.

任何重量的損失超過百分之二以上，我們都會補償。

**

offhand〔'ɔf'hænd〕*adv.* 即刻地
shipment〔'ʃɪpmənt〕*n.* 裝船
transportation〔,trænspə'teʃən〕*n.* 運輸
compensate〔'kɑmpən,set〕*v.* 賠償

short ton 美噸（2,000 磅）

❋ 交易價格 ❋

♧ What about the cost of delivery?

運費怎麼算？

♧ On what terms?

在什麼條件下？

♧ We'd like to do it *in accordance with* an F.O.B. con-
tract.

我們想依照 F.O.B. 契約（來
算）。

♧ How much is the export
price?

輸出價格是多少？

♧ We offer this article at US
$200 per unit C.I.F. Se-
attle.

這項產品以 C.I.F. 算，送到
西雅圖，我們出價每台兩百美
元。

♧ *Are all the quotations C.I.
F.?*

所有的報價，都以 C.I.F. 來
算嗎？

❋ 減價 ❋

♧ I'd like to discuss the price.

我想討論一下價格。

♧ What about discounts and
terms of sale?

折扣和銷售條件是怎麼樣的？

**— ──────────────

F.O.B. 船上交貨價（= *free on board*）
C.I.F. 運費及保費在內價（= *cost, insurance, and freight*）
quotation〔kwoʼteʃən〕*n.* 估價；報價

♤ The prices and discounts are pro-　價格和折扣，對我們而言
blems for us.　是個問題。

♤ That's a little more than we　那有點兒高於我們預期要
were expecting to pay.　付的價格。

♤ That's too high.　（ 價錢 ）太高了。

♤ Will you make it a little cheaper?　可不可以便宜一點？

♤ Can't you quote us anything　您能不能開價便宜一點？
cheaper?

♤ Will you reduce the cost?　可不可以降低價格？

♤ *Can't you make it cheaper*?　您不能算便宜一點嗎？

♤ Could you give us *more of a dis-*　您能不能多給我們一點折
count?　扣？

♤ How much do you think you　您想您能降價多少？
could *bring* the price *down*?

♤ Is this your *best* price?　這是您最徹底的價錢了嗎？

♤ How about $180 per unit?　每台美金一百八十元怎麼
樣？

♤ Please cut the price down to　請降價到每台美金一百八
$180 per unit.　十元。

** ————————————————

bring down 使降低

best 〔bɛst〕*adj*. 最好的；最有用（利）的；夠徹底的

♤ A German manufacturer has offered us a price ten percent lower than yours.　　有一家德國廠商給我們出的價，比你們的低了百分之十。

♤ They have just announced a ten percent reduction in their price.　　他們剛才宣佈減價百分之十。

♤ Expensive units won't sell in our market.　　我們的市場，高價位的東西賣不出去。

♤ If you won't come down to $35,000, we won't buy one.　　如果你們不降到美金三萬五千元，我們一台也不買。

❊ 希望以大量採購獲得折扣 ❊

♤ Can you *offer a quantity discount*?　　你們能提供大量訂購的折扣嗎？

♤ If we order 1,000 units or more, how much can you bring the price down?　　如果我們訂一千台，或者更多，你們能降價多少？

♤ What would happen to the price if we doubled the order?　　如果我們加倍訂購，價錢怎麼算？

♤ What discount can you offer for orders over $100,000 *net*?　　訂貨超過實價十萬美元的話，你們能提供怎麼樣的折扣？

---

announce〔əˋnaʊns〕v. 發表；宣布　　reduction〔rɪˋdʌkʃən〕n. 減少
net〔nɛt〕n. 實價；淨利；實重

❋ 打算給與客戶折扣 ❋

♤ Then, *we'll make it* $5.50. 　　那麼,我們算美金五元五角。

♤ We can bring the price down to $380 per unit. 　　我們可以降價到每台三百八十美元。

♤ We'll *make a ten percent discount*. 　　我們可以打九折。

♤ Ten percent might be possible. 　　九折也許可以。

♤ If you order a large quantity, I think a discount would be possible. 　　如果您大量訂購,我想也許可以打折。

♤ If you order 100 units or more, you will *recieve* a ten percent discount. 　　如果您訂一百台或者更多,可享九折優待。

♤ We'd be ready to give you a three percent special discount, if you order 100 units or more. 　　如果您訂一百台或者更多的話,我們準備給您百分之三的特別折扣。

♤ What price do you think would *make it competitive*? 　　您認為什麼樣的價格,可以經得起競爭?

♤ I'll ask the main office to accept a discount. 　　我會要求總公司接受折扣。

＊＊────────────────

competitive〔kəm'pɛtətɪv〕*adj.* 競爭的;經得起競爭的

✳ 表示很難再減價 ✳

♤ This is the lowest possible price.　這是可能的最低價了。

♤ The price is quite reasonable.　這價格是相當合理的。

♤ The most we can offer is $38,000.　我們最多能出（價）美金三萬八。

♤ Ten percent wouldn't be worthwhile for my company.　九折對本公司不划算。

♤ Raw material prices have risen, so we can't sell our product at that price.　原料費漲了，因此我們的產品不能以那個價錢賣。

♤ We're selling *at cost* already.　我們已經是以成本在賣了。

♤ We're already quoting our lowest price.　我們已經開出最低價了。

♤ We *cannot make any further discount*.　我們不能再打折了。

♤ Our prices are supposed to be much lower than other companies.　我們的價格應該比其他公司低很多了。

---

reasonable〔'riznəbḷ〕*adj.* 合理的；公道的
worthwhile〔'wɝθ'hwaɪl〕*adj.* 值得的

♤ I'm afraid that there is no *room* to *negotiate* the price. 　　　　恐怕沒有商議價格的餘地了。

♤ My boss says we can't negotiate the price any further. 　　　　我老板說，價錢我們不能再商議了。

❋ 價格變動 ❋

♤ Will the prices vary? 　　　　價格會變動嗎？

♤ Prices have risen. 　　　　價格漲了。

♤ Prices have fallen. 　　　　價格跌了。

♤ The price has stayed the same. 　　　　價格一樣。

♤ The price has gone up $8.50 per unit. 　　　　每台的價格上漲了美金八元五角。

♤ The price has gone down $8.50 per unit. 　　　　每台的價格跌了美金八元五角。

♤ We had to raise the price because the cost of raw materials rose. 　　　　由於原料價格上漲，我們必須漲價。

♤ Please let us know as soon as the price changes. 　　　　價格一變動，請立刻通知我們。

** ─────────────

room〔rum〕*n.* 餘地；機會　　negotiate〔nɪˈgoʃɪˌet〕*v.* 商議
vary〔ˈvɛrɪ〕*v.* 變動；修改

♤ *Please let us know in detail* about price changes.

關於價格的變動，請詳細告訴我們。

♤ Prices may vary, without notice, in accordance with *market fluc-tuations*.

依照市場的波動，價格可能在不可預知的情況下變動。

♤ We'll sell it this time *at* the old price.

這次我們全照老價錢賣。

** ────────────────────

fluctuation 〔ˌflʌktʃʊˈeʃən〕 *n.* 不停的變動；波動

UNIT 2

Discussing the payment
談付款

<對話精華>

· We usually do business **in dollars**.
　我們通常用美元來做生意。

· As everyone knows, the exchange rate **fluctuates** almost daily.
　如大家所知，滙率幾乎每天都在不停的變動。

· You can pay **on a ten month installment plan**.
　您可以分十個月來分期付款。

※ 討論滙率的問題 ※

♤ How do you intend to **handle** the exchange rate problem?

您打算如何處理滙率問題？

♤ **Regarding** payment, what do you have in mind for dealing with the problem of exchange rates?

關於付款，在處理滙率問題方面，您有什麼意見呢？

---

exchange rate 滙率
payment〔'pemənt〕*n.* 支付；付出之款

♤ We usually do business *in dollars*. 　我們通常用美元來做生意。

♤ As far as the base price is concerned, we want to do it in NT dollars. 　就基本價格而言，我們希望用新台幣。

♤ We'd like to pay in NT dollars. 　我們想付新台幣。

♤ Our policy has been to deal *in terms of* NT dollars. 　我們的方針，一直是以新台幣爲交易方式。

♤ We have to pay for manufacturing in NT dollars. 　我們必須以新台幣付製造費。

♤ We will be selling your product in NT dollars. 　我們將以新台幣，來賣你們的產品。

♤ As everyone knows, the exchange rate *fluctuates* almost daily. 　如大家所知，滙率幾乎每天都在不停的變動。

♤ A one-cent or two-cent price fluctuation is not serious, but if the exchange rate fluctuates more we'll be in trouble. 　一分或二分價格的變動並不嚴重，但是如果滙率變動太大，我們就有麻煩了。

♤ Since world prices are often dollar based, I think we should *pay in dollars*. 　因爲全世界價格常以美元做基礎，我想我們應該以美元來付。

**──────────────

dollar 〔ˈdɑlɚ〕 *n.* 元，通常指「 美元 」而言　　*in terms of* 以…的方式
fluctuate 〔ˈflʌktʃʊ͵et〕 *v.* 波動；不停的變動

♤ Let's decide on the rate each time you order.   每次您訂貨時，我們就來決定利率。

♤ Let's negotiate the price when it goes up or down two cents.   價格上升或下降兩分時，我們就來商議價格。

❋ 談付款的條件 ❋

♤ Would you please tell us the terms of payment?   請您告訴我們付款的條件好嗎？

♤ What are the *terms of payment*?   付款的條件是什麼？

♤ What are your terms?   你們的條件是什麼？

♤ You will need to *open* an L/C (letter of credit).   您將必須開信用狀。

♤ Will you open L/Cs for initial orders?   剛開始訂的貨，請您開信用狀好嗎？

❋ 談付款期限 ❋

♤ When can we expect payment?   我們何時可以收款？

♤ We expect payment in advance on first orders.   我們希望第一次訂的貨，能先付款。

---

terms〔tɝmz〕*n.* 條件　　L/C 信用狀（= *letter of credit*）
initial〔ɪˈnɪʃəl〕*adj.* 最初的，開始的

♤ When you place the first order we expect thirty percent of the final payment.

您第一次訂貨時，我們希望先收到總款數的百分之三十。

♤ Please pay us within sixty days *from* the invoice date.

請在開發票六十天之內付款。

♤ We'll send our bill at the end of each month, so please pay by the end of *the following month*.

我們會在每個月底寄帳單，所以請在次月的月底之前付款。

♤ We ask for a ten percent payment when you order.

我們要求訂貨時，先交百分之十的款數。

♤ You can *pay on a ten month install-ment plan*.

您可以分十個月來分期付款。

♤ We ask for a twenty percent *down payment*.

我們要求百分之二十的頭期款。

♤ You can pay the rest in ten monthly installments.

其餘的您可以分十個月來分期付款。

♤ We'd like to talk about credit.

我們想談談貸款的事。

♤ Could you supply us with initial stock *on* three months credit?

剛開始的貨品，您能給我們三個月的信用貸款嗎？

---

invoice〔'ɪnvɔɪs〕*v.* 開發票　　installment〔ɪn'stɔlmənt〕*n.* 分期付款
down payment 分期付款的頭期款　　credit〔'krɛdɪt〕*n.* 信用；貸款

UNIT 3

Discussing minimum orders, commissions & advertisement fees
談訂貨量・佣金・廣告費

＜對話精華＞

- How about *a ten percent commission*?
  百分之十的佣金怎麼樣？

- Is that a *flat* ten percent? 是不是都固定百分之十？

- We require *a fifty-fifty split on the expenses*.
  我們需要平均分攤費用。

❋ 談訂貨數量 ❋

♠ *Regarding* inventory, we'd like you to keep three months' worth of stock *on hand*.

關於存貨，我們希望你們保留三個月現有的存貨。

♤ *Concerning* inventory, would you please keep four months' worth of stock on hand?

關於存貨，請您保留四個月現有的存貨好嗎？

♠ Please order 1,000 units *in bulk*.

請大量訂購一千台。

❋❋ ─────────────────

inventory 〔ˈɪnvənˌtorɪ〕*n.* 存貨；清單上開列之貨品
on hand 現有　　*in bulk* 大量；批發

♠ That would *tie up* a considerable amount of capital.

那會省下一筆可觀的資金。

♠ Do you suppose 500 units
would be sufficient?

您認爲五百台夠嗎？

♠ We don't like to have too much
stock on hand.

我們不喜歡有太多現有的存
貨。

♠ Could you wait a little longer
for your payment from us?

可否請您延緩我們付款的時
間？

♠ If we have to order 1,000
units at a time we must *ask
for a delay in payment*.

如果我們一次要訂一千台，
我們想要求延期付款。

※ 談佣金的支付 ※

♠ We'll provide you a commission
on sales.

我們會給付您買賣的佣金。

♠ What's the agency commission
rate?

代理商佣金的比例是多少？

♠ We normally pay a twelve percent commission on *net sales*.

我們通常付實價買賣百分之
十二的佣金。

♠ How much commission do you
expect?

您希望多少佣金？

---

tie up 省 (錢) 不用；留起 (財物) 不用　　capital 〔'kæpətḷ〕 *n.* 資金；資本

♤ How about *a ten percent com-mission*?　　　　　　　　　　　百分之十的佣金怎麼樣？

♤ Does that mean you'll pay a ten percent commission on every or-der from Taiwan?　　　　　是不是說每次從台灣訂貨，您都付百分之十的佣金？

♤ Is that a *flat* ten percent?　　　　是不是都固定百分之十？

♤ Does that price include our commission?　　　　　　　　　那個價錢有包含我們的佣金嗎？

♤ We really can't sell your prod-ucts at that commission rate.　　我們實在無法以那個佣金比例來銷售你們的產品。

♤ How will you pay the commission?　　您要怎麼支付佣金？

♤ We'll pay a monthly sales com-mission at the end of the follow-ing month.　　　　　　　　每個月買賣的佣金，我們會在次月的月底支付。

♤ We'll calculate the commission for monthly sales.　　　　　我們會每個月計算買賣的佣金。

♤ We'll pay the commission two months later on the fifteenth.　　我們會在兩個月後的十五號給付佣金。

♤ The commission will be trans-fered to your *bank account*.　　佣金會轉到您銀行裏的戶頭。

---

flat〔flæt〕*adj*. 固定的　　calculate〔'kælkjə,let〕*v*. 計算；估計

❋ 談廣告費用的分攤 ❋

♤ Is it possible for you to *back us up* with a reasonable *amount* of advertising?

你們可不可能支持我們相當程度的廣告費？

♤ For products of this kind, the quality of advertising determines the sales.

這類的產品，廣告的品質決定了銷售數量。

♤ How could you help us?

你們能怎樣幫我們？

♤ I'm afraid we can't pay for your *sales promotion* expenses.

恐怕我們不能支付你們促銷的費用。

♤ How about your company paying for some of the costs?

你們公司負擔--部份費用怎麼樣？

♤ The cost of advertising being as high as it is these days, we couldn't *absorb* the total expense for it.

最近廣告費太高了，我們無法負擔全部的費用。

♤ We can't *cover* the total cost of advertising.

我們無法負擔全部的廣告費。

♤ The *promotion* of this product will benefit the both of us.

這項產品的促銷，對我們雙方都有利。

---

back up 支持；擁護　　amount〔ə'maʊnt〕n. 數量；程度；範圍
promotion〔prə'moʃən〕n.〔由宣傳〕促進銷售
absorb〔əb'sɔrb〕v. 負擔

♧ Do you have any idea how much it'll be?
您知不知道要多少錢？

♧ We require *a fifty-fifty split on the expenses.*
我們需要平均分攤費用。

♧ I'm sure it will benefit you just the same.
我確信那將同樣對您有利。

♧ Our *share* will be about $5,000 a month.
我們每月大約分攤五千美元。

♧ We usually ask for fifteen percent of the total monthly whole sale figures.
我們通常要求，每月總銷售額的百分之十五。

♧ We could *settle* for ten percent of the monthly whole sale prices.
我們可以償付每月總銷售價的百分之十。

♧ We're prepared to provide technical assistance in the initial stages.
剛開始的階段，我們打算提供技術援助。

♧ Concerning the warranty, we will absorb *up to* three percent of the annual gross sales figures.
關於保證金，我們會負擔高達每年總銷售額的百分之三。

**

split〔splɪt〕*v*. 分配　　figure〔'fɪgɚ〕*n*. 價錢
settle〔'setḷ〕*v*. 清算；償付　　*up to* 高達
gross〔gros〕*adj*. 總共的　　*n*. 總數；總計

UNIT 4

After-sales service
售後服務

<對話精華>

- What's the warranty **on** this machine？
  這部機器有什麼擔保？
- This machine **carries** a five-year warranty.
  這部機器有五年的保證。
- All repairs will be made **free of charge** during the warranty period.
  在保證期間內，所有的修理都是免費的。

※ 關於保證期間 ※

♤ What's your policy on warranty？　　你們的保證方針是什麼？

♤ What's the warranty on this ma-　　這部機器有什麼擔保？
chine？

♤ How long is the warranty on this　　這部機器的保證期有多
machine？　　久？

♤ We'll guarantee it for two years.　　（這個）我們保證兩年。

**

warranty〔'wɔrəntɪ〕*n.* 保證；擔保契約

♤ We'll give it a three-year warranty. | 這個我們給予三年的保證。

♤ This machine **carries a five-year warranty**. | 這部機器有五年的保證。

♤ We provide a full warranty for a period of six months. | 我們提供爲期六個月的完全保證。

♤ Is it possible to **extend** the period of warranty? | 有可能延長保證期嗎？

♤ I want you to guarantee it for at least three years. | 我要您至少保證三年。

♤ A competing company has offered a three-year warranty. | 一家競爭的公司，提供了三年的保證。

✳ 關於售後服務 ✳

♤ We have some questions about **after-sales service**. | 關於售後服務我們有些問題。

♤ We'll send a person to explain how to operate the machine. | 我們會派人去說明，怎麼操作機器。

♤ Our service center is located near your company. | 我們的服務中心，就在你們公司附近。

＊＊

operate 〔'ɑpə,ret〕 *v.* 操縱

♤ This machine can be repaired at any service center in the States.

這部機器，可以在美國任何一家服務中心修理。

♤ If there is any trouble in the future we will give quick service.

如果將來有任何問題，我們會提供快速的服務。

♤ We have trained and experienced engineers in our service centers.

本服務中心有受過訓練，經驗豐富的技師。

♤ We'll visit you for maintenance checks *on a monthly basis*.

我們會每個月爲您做保養檢查。

✳ 關於修理費用 ✳

♤ We'll provide regular maintenance checks *free of charge*.

我們會免費地提供定期的保養檢查。

♤ All repairs will be made free of charge during the warranty period.

保證期間內，所有的修理都是免費的。

♤ The warranty also provides *free labor* for service calls during the warranty period.

保證在保期內，同時也提供免費的修理服務。

♤ We may have to *charge for a repair* if it's determined that you've used the machine improperly.

如果確定是您沒按標準使用機器的話，我們也許要收修理費。

---

maintenance 〔'mentənəns〕 *n*. 保養

♤ What about after the warranty expires?

保證期滿之後怎麼樣呢？

♤ All repairs are billed *at cost*.

所有的修理都照成本收費。

♤ We'll bill you for *parts*.

我們是記您零件的帳。

♤ We usually bill for service calls *by* the hour.

我們通常以小時來計算服務費。

❋ 詢問設備的租借條件 ❋

♤ Will you offer us *the same* service policy on leased equipment *as* on purchased equipment?

租用設備，您是否提供和購買設備相同的服務？

♤ How do you handle your pricing for your *leased equipment*?

您如何處理您出租設備的價格？

♤ How will you charge for leased equipment with options?

出租設備的選擇您如何索價?

♤ Are service calls free of charge during the lease period?

在租期內，修理服務是不是免費的呢？

＊＊
expire〔ɪk'spaɪr〕*v.* 滿期；終止　　　bill〔bɪl〕*v.* 記入帳；送帳單給
lease〔lis〕*v.* 出租　　purchase〔'pɝtʃəs〕*v.* 購買
option〔'ɑpʃən〕*n.* 選擇權；選擇之事物

Vocabulary Street 付款・價格專用術語

- □ pay in one lump sum 一次總付
- □ pay in installments 分期付款
- □ first installment 分期付款的首次款（= *first payment* ）
- □ credit memo 欠款通知
- □ pay by check 付支票　　pay cash 付現金

～～～～～～～～～～～～～～～

- □ total price 總價　　fixed price 不二價
- □ fair price 公平價格　　average price 平均價格
- □ half price 半價（優待）　　bottom price 最底價
- □ rock-bottom prices 血本（= *net cost* ）
- □ special price 特價　　wholesale price 批發價

～～～～～～～～～～～～～～～

- □ trade discount 同行折扣　　inventory sale 存貨減價
- □ commodity price 物價　　price fluctuation 物價波動
- □ current price 時價　　regular price 原價
- □ market price 市價　　general（price）increase 一般漲價
- □ big discount 大削售　　price cutting 削價
- □ EOM（End-of-the-Month）Sale 月終大廉價
- □ season sale 季節減價　　year-end sale 年終大廉價
- □ clearance sale 清倉廉價
- □ opening price 開市價（= *initial price* ）

商談・簽約
基礎會話

CHAPTER
VII

1. 商談時的各類狀況
2. 如何議定契約與訂約

UNIT 1

Business discussions of all situations
商談時的各類狀況

<對話精華>

· **Let's get down to business**, shall we?
  我們開始談事了，好嗎？

· **I'm against it**. 我反對。

· We can't be **flexible** on this point.
  關於這點，我們不能讓步。

※ 要開始商談時 ※

℧ Let's **get down** to business, shall we?   我們開始談事了，好嗎？

℧ Shall we begin?   我們可以開始了嗎？

℧ Perhaps we should begin.   或許我們應該開始了。

℧ Well, how shall we begin?   嗯，我們要怎麼開始呢？

℧ Where shall we begin?   我們從哪裏開始？

℧ How shall we **proceed**?   我們要怎麼開始進行？

**

proceed〔prə'sid〕*v.* 進行；開始進行

☃ Where shall we start our discussion today?

我們今天的討論要從哪裏開始？

☃ What part of the contract should we discuss?

我們該討論合約中的哪個部分？

❈ 同意對方的意見 ❈

☃ I agree (with you). — 我同意（您）。

☃ Exactly. — 對極了。

☃ Very true. — 非常正確。

☃ (You're) quite right. — （您）對極了。

☃ I suppose you're right. — 我想您是對的。

☃ That's true. — 的確。

☃ That's correct. — 對的。

☃ That's right. — 對的。

☃ That's very good. — 太好了。

☃ OK, that will be fine. — 好，那樣可以。

☃ That's a good idea. — 這是個好主意。

☃ Sure. Good idea. — 的確，好主意。

☃ That *sounds* reasonable to me. — 聽起來很合理。

☃ Fair enough. — 很公平。

☃ That seems OK. — 那似乎還可以。

ℭ I'm sure *that's the case*. 　　　我確信就是這樣。

ℭ *That makes sense*. 　　　很合理。

ℭ I agree with you up to that 　　　關於那點，我同意您的看
point. 　　　法。

ℭ I see what you mean and I 　　　我懂您的意思，而且我也
appreciate your position. 　　　很清楚您的立場。

ℭ Yes, I understand your point of 　　　是的，我明白您的觀點。
view.

ℭ I can appreciate your concern. 　　　我察覺得到您所憂慮的。

ℭ I can understand your situation. 　　　我可以了解您的立場。

ℭ Oh, yes. That's very important. 　　　喔,是的。那是非常重要的。

ℭ Right. That's essential. 　　　對，那是很重要的。

ℭ I'd like that very much. 　　　那點我很贊同。

ℭ Sure, *I'd be delighted*. 　　　當然，我很高興。

ℭ Yes, I'm sure we can. 　　　是的，我確信我們可以。

ℭ That would be just fine. 　　　那很好。

ℭ We'd like to accept your pro- 　　　我們願意接受您的提議。
posal.

＊＊――――――――――――――

case〔kes〕*n.* 令人信服的理論；情形；狀況　　*make sense* 合理；理解
appreciate〔ə'priʃɪ,et〕*v.* 賞識；察知；辨別
essential〔ə'sɛnʃəl〕*adj.* 重要的；必要的　　proposal〔prə'pozḷ〕*n.* 提議

※ 對對方的意見給予不明確的答覆 ※

౮ That may be.   也許吧 。

౮ Yes, maybe that's the best   是的，也許那是最好的主意。
idea.

౮ ***That depends.***   看情形而定 。

౮ It's possible.   可能吧 。

౮ I'm not sure.   我不確定 。

※ 反對對方的意見 ※

౮ I don't agree with you.   我不贊同您的意見 。

౮ ***I'm against it***.   我反對 。

౮ I can't agree.   我無法贊同 。

౮ I'm opposed to the idea.   那個意見我反對 。

౮ I don't think that's a good   我認爲那不是個好主意 。
idea.

౮ I don't think so.   我不這麼認爲 。

---

oppose〔ə'poz〕*v.* 反對

❀ 拒絕對方的提議 ❀

⊗ I'm afraid I can't accept your proposal.

恐怕我不能接受您的提議。

⊗ We're not prepared at this time to accept your proposal.

我們現在還不準備接受您的提議。

⊗ I'm afraid we can't accept your *offer* because the price is *much higher than* our estimate.

恐怕我們無法接受您出的價，因為價格比我們預估的高得多。

❀ 希望對方重新考慮 ❀

⊗ Could you reconsider the terms of payment?

您能再考慮一下付款條件嗎？

⊗ Could you think about the terms of payment again?

您能再考慮考慮付款條件嗎？

⊗ Isn't there any way to change your plans?

沒有辦法改變您的計畫了嗎？

⊗ I'd like you to think about this problem *one more time.*

這個問題，我希望您再考慮一次。

⊗ *We can't be flexible* on this point.

關於這點，我們不能讓步。

**————

estimate 〔'ɛstəmɪt〕 *n*. 評價；估計
reconsider 〔͵rikən'sɪdɚ〕 *v*. 再考慮
flexible 〔'flɛksəbl̩〕 *adj*. 易說服的；可修改的

❈ 不能明確地答覆時 ❈

♋ Please let me think it over. 　　請讓我考慮看看。

♋ This is something we have to consider. 　　這就是我們要考慮的。

♋ Would it be all right to give you an answer tomorrow? 　　明天給您答覆可以嗎？

♋ It's impossible for me to give *a definite answer* now. 　　我現在無法給予一個明確的答覆。

♋ It's not my decision. 　　這不是我能決定的。

♋ I need time to *consult with* my colleagues. 　　我需要時間和我同事商量一下。

♋ I can't *reach* a decision by myself at this time. 　　這時候，我無法自己做決定。

♋ *I don't have the authority to* decide on this alone. 　　這個我無權自己決定。

♋ I will *convey* your request *to* upper management. 　　我會把您的要求，傳達給上面的主管。

---

colleague〔'kɑlig〕*n.* 同事　　convey〔kən've〕*v.* 通知；傳達

※ 詢問對方的意見 ※

උ I'd like to hear your ideas about the problem.

我想聽聽您對這個問題的意見。

උ If I knew your opinion, it would be very helpful.

如果我能知道您的意見，會是非常有幫助的。

උ Let me have your views about this project.

讓我知道您對於這個計畫的看法。

උ We would like to have your *candid* opinion.

我們想知道您真正的看法。

උ Are there any other comments?

有任何其他的意見嗎？

උ Any opinions?

有任何意見嗎？

උ What do you think, Mr. Scott?

史考特先生,您認為如何呢？

උ What are your feelings about this report?

關於這個報告，您覺得如何？

උ What's your *immediate reaction* to this report?

對於這個報告，您第一個反應是什麼？

උ What's your opinion of the proposal?

這個提議,您有什麼看法？

**※ ————————————————

project〔'prɑdʒɛkt〕*n.* 計畫；設計
candid〔'kændɪd〕*adj.* 坦白的；公正的；真實的
comment〔'kɑmɛnt〕*n.* 批評；意見

♡ What do you propose we do?　　　　您建議我們怎麼做？

♡ Do you agree to this?　　　　　　這個您同意嗎？

♡ Are there any *objections*?　　　　有沒有異議？

♡ Thank you for expressing your　　謝謝您表達您的意見。
opinion.

✷ 不明白對方的意思時 ✷

♡ *I beg your pardon*?　　　　　　　再說一次好嗎？

♡ (Beg your) pardon?　　　　　　　再說一次好嗎？

♡ Would you mind repeating it?　　　您介意再說一次嗎？

♡ What did you say?　　　　　　　　您（剛才）說什麼？

♡ I'm sorry I didn't quite *follow*　　很抱歉，我不太懂您的意
you.　　　　　　　　　　　　　思。

♡ I'm sorry, but I don't under-　　　很抱歉，我聽不懂。
stand.

♡ I'm sorry, I'm not sure I un-　　　很抱歉，我不確定我是不
derstand your point.　　　　　　是瞭解您的意思。

♡ Could you be more specific?　　　您能說得更明確一點嗎？

**

propose〔prə'poz〕*v*. 建議　　objection〔əb'dʒɛkʃən〕*n*. 異議
specific〔spɪ'sɪfɪk〕*adj*. 明確的

ℭ Could you please **put it more briefly**? 您能說得更簡短一點嗎？

ℭ Could you tell us about it **in more detail**? 關於這個，您能跟我們說得更詳細一點嗎？

ℭ Could you explain it more precisely for us? 您能把這個解釋得更明確一點嗎？

ℭ Could you explain what you mean? 您能解釋一下您的意思嗎？

ℭ Please explain it again. 請再解釋一遍。

❈ 表示意見・提出問題 ❈

ℭ Let me tell you what I think. 讓我告訴您我的想法。

ℭ Let me express my opinion. 讓我表達我的意見。

ℭ May I ask a question? 我可以問個問題嗎？

ℭ May I ask another question? 我可以再問個問題嗎？

ℭ **Just one more question.** 再問一個問題。

❈ 強調互相合作 ❈

ℭ We'd like for you to **have confidence in** us. 我們希望您能信任我們。

------

precisely〔prɪˈsaɪslɪ〕*adv*. 正確地；精確地
confidence〔ˈkɑnfədəns〕*n*. 信任

♡ We'll do our best to *meet* your 　　我們會盡所能來滿足您的
　　demands. 　　　　　　　　　　　需求。

♡ We ask for your cooperation. 　　　我們需要您的合作。

♡ We know we can *count on* you. 　　我們知道我們可以信賴您。

♡ We need your cooperation. 　　　　我們需要您的合作。

♡ I know, we both want the best 　　　我知道，我們雙方都希望
　　possible arrangement. 　　　　　　有最好的處理。

✲ 有必須研討的地方 ✲

♡ We have some points we need to 　　有些項目，我們需要再進
　　explore further. 　　　　　　　　一步研討。

♡ There are some points that need 　　有些項目需要再研究。
　　to be worked out.

♡ There are some points that we 　　有些項目我們還沒解決。
　　haven't settled yet.

♡ *There is some necessity* for 　　　有些細節是需要討論的。
　　discussion on some of the finer
　　points.

✲✲ ───────────────────────────

　　cooperation〔ko͵ɑpəˈreʃən〕*n.* 合作；協力
　　arrangement〔əˈrendʒmənt〕*n.* 安排；處理
　　explore〔ɪkˈsplor〕*v.* 研究

❋ 表示不滿意 ❋

ε♂ Are you satisfied with all the points?　　　　　　　　　　所有的論點您都滿意嗎？

ε♂ There are a few points we can't accept.　　　　　　　　有些論點我們不能接受。

ε♂ We're not entirely satisfied with the terms of payment.　　我們並不完全滿意付款的條件。

ε♂ We feel the terms of payment are a bit *stiff*.　　　　　　我們覺得付款條件有點嚴苛。

ε♂ Your terms of payment are too severe.　　　　　　　　你們付款的條件太嚴苛了。

ε♂ We haven't agreed on *publicity expenses* yet.　　　　　　關於宣傳費，我們還沒同意。

ε♂ We need to agree on publicity expenses.　　　　　　　　關於宣傳費，我們必須達成協議。

ε♂ Our lawyers have some questions about the terms of payment.　我們的律師對於付款條件有些疑問。

＊＊

stiff〔stɪf〕*adj.* 嚴厲的；過分的
severe〔sə'vɪr〕*adj.* 嚴厲的；苛刻的
publicity〔pʌb'lɪsətɪ〕*n.* 廣告；宣傳；出風頭

❀ 確認同意之項目 ❀

🕭 Let me summarize our discussion.　　讓我概述一下我們討論的。

🕭 Let's review what's been decided on so far.　　讓我們重覆一下，目前已經決定的事。

🕭 Let's re-establish the points we agree on.　　讓我們再確定一下我們已經同意的項目。

🕭 Before the formal contract is drawn up we'd like to restate the main points of the agreement.　　在草擬正式合約之前，我們再重述一次我們協議的主要項目。

🕭 We've agreed on the price of $125 per unit.　　我們已同意每台一百二十五美元的價格。

🕭 We're *in accord* on these points, aren't we?　　我們一致同意這些項目，不是嗎？

🕭 We've agreed on price and terms of payment.　　我們已同意了價格和付款條件。

🕭 We've agreed on all the basic points.　　所有的基本項目我們已經同意。

🕭 We're in agreement on all points.　　所有的項目，我們都達成了協議。

🕭 We're in complete agreement.　　我們完全達成協議。

❊❊─────────────

summarize〔'sʌmə‚raɪz〕*v.* 摘要；概述　　***draw up*** 草擬

☃ I think *we've arrived at* a mutually satisfactory agreement. 　　我想我們已達到雙方都滿意的協議。

※ 中途退席 ※

☃ Excuse me, I have an important phone call. 　　對不起，我有一通重要的電話。

☃ Excuse me, I have to *answer* the phone. 　　對不起，我必須接個電話。

☃ I'm really sorry, but I have to leave. 　　眞的很抱歉，我必須走了。

☃ Please excuse me for a moment. 　　對不起，失陪一下。

☃ Excuse me, I'll be back in a moment. 　　對不起，我馬上回來。

☃ Excuse me, I'll be back in ten minutes. 　　對不起，我十分鐘後就回來。

☃ Excuse me, I'll be back at three. 　　對不起，我三點會回來。

※ 商談結束時 ※

☃ I think we can *go into more detail* at our next meeting. 　　我想下次的會議，我們可以討論得更詳細一點。

☃ Let's discuss it more tomorrow. 　　我們明天再多討論一點。

☃ *Let's call it a day today.* 　　今天到此爲止。

UNIT 2

Discussing the terms of the contract & signing the contract
如何議定契約與訂約

< 對話精華 >

· Shall we ***draw up*** a draft of the contract?
　我們要不要草擬一份契約草案?

· This contract is ***valid*** for three years.
　這份契約有效期三年。

· ***With three months' notice*** the contract can ***be annulled***. 三個月的公告,合約便可廢止。

❈ 關於契約 ❈

☯ We're looking forward to discussing a contract with you.　　　我們期待和您討論契約。

☯ We'd like to discuss an agency contract with you.　　　我們想和您討論代理商契約。

☯ I'd like to talk about an ***exclusive*** agreement.　　　我想談談獨家(代理商)契約。

**

contract〔ˈkɑntrækt〕*n.* 合約
exclusive〔ɪkˈsklusɪv〕*adj.* 獨有的

℧ When can we meet to discuss the contract?   我們何時可以見個面討論契約？

℧ Let's **make** a contract as soon as possible.   讓我們儘快訂契約。

℧ Let's talk about the contract.   讓我們來談談契約。

❈ 有關契約草案 ❈

℧ Shall we **draw up** a draft of the contract?   我們要不要草擬一份契約草案？

℧ We'll prepare a draft of the contract.   我們會準備一份契約草案。

℧ This is our standard contract.   這是我們標準的契約。

℧ We'll prepare a draft according to our (standard) contract.   我們會根據我們標準的契約，準備一份草案。

℧ We'll send you a draft of the contract in the mail.   我們會寄給您一份契約草案。

℧ After the draft is completed, we can work out any minor problems.   草案完成後，我們就可以解決其他較小的問題。

---

draft〔dræft〕*n.* 草稿   standard〔'stændəd〕*n.* 標準
work out 解決（問題）；精細計劃

᠔ Have you seen the draft of the contract? 您看過合約草案了嗎？

᠔ We've received the draft of the contract. 我們已收到契約草稿。

᠔ Please examine the draft as quickly as you can. 請您儘快檢視一下草案。

❈ 討論契約的各項細目 ❈

᠔ Let's discuss the warranty. 讓我們來討論保證的事。

᠔ *The first point we should discuss is* how we pay for the *publicity expenses.* 我們該討論的第一點是如何付宣傳費。

᠔ We'd like to discuss the details of the contract. 我們想討論契約的各項細目。

᠔ We'd like to discuss the terms of payment in more detail. 我們想更詳細地討論付款條件。

᠔ We'd like to talk about the warranty a little more. 我們想多談談有關保證的事。

᠔ We'd like to talk in more detail about the procedure for starting sales. 我們想更詳細地談談開賣的程序。

---

warranty 〔'wɔrəntɪ〕 *n.* 保證；擔保   procedure 〔prə'sidʒɚ〕 *n.* 程序

❋ 商談契約期限 ❋

☺ How long will the contract last?　契約要訂多長？

☺ How long shall we make the contract for?　契約要訂多久？

☺ Initially, it would *run* for one year, a kind of *trial period*.　剛開始是一年，算是試驗期。

☺ We feel that a one-year contract is too short.　我們覺得一年的契約太短了。

☺ We'd like to make a three-year contract.　我們想訂三年的契約。

☺ This contract is *valid* for three years.　這份契約有效期三年。

☺ If everything is satisfactory, it could be renewed and extended two years.　如果事事都令人滿意，契約可以重訂，而且延長兩年。

☺ The contract will be renewed annually.　契約將每年重訂一次。

☺ *If both sides agree*, the contract can be renewed annually.　如果雙方同意，契約可以每年重訂一次。

---

initially〔ɪˋnɪʃəlɪ〕*adv.* 開始地　　valid〔ˋvælɪd〕*adj.* 有效的
renew〔rɪˋnju〕*v.* 更新；重訂　　annually〔ˋænjʊəlɪ〕*adv.* 一年一次地

❋ 變更合約內容‧取消合約 ❋

℘ Is it possible to change the details of the contract after it's made?

可不可能在契約訂立後，更改細節？

℘ The details of the contract can be changed **only when** both partners agree to the change.

合約的細節，只有在雙方同意更改之下才能修改。

℘ Is it possible to cancel the contract while it's **in effect**?

可不可能在生效的時候取消合約？

℘ The contract can be cancelled by mutual agreement.

契約在雙方同意之下可以取消。

℘ **With three months' notice** the contract can **be annulled**.

三個月的公告，合約便可廢止。

❋ 正式簽約 ❋

℘ If everything is satisfactory, we can draw up a formal contract.

如果事事都令人滿意，我們可以正式簽約。

℘ Please contact me as soon as you're ready to sign.

您一準備好簽約時，請儘快通知我。

---

cancel〔ˈkænsḷ〕v. 作廢；取消　　**in effect** 實際上；有效；生效
annul〔əˈnʌl〕v. 廢止

♔ We'll look over this contract in Taipei.

我們會在台北，再校閱一次這份契約。

♔ I'll have my president look at this contract.

我會請我們董事長，看看這份契約。

♔ When will the contract papers be ready?

合約書何時可準備好？

♔ When can we sign the contract?

我們何時可以簽約？

♔ We expect to have a final contract ready in a week.

我們希望一週內，可準備好正式的合約書。

♔ I'll prepare the contract right away.

我會馬上準備契約。

♔ We except to make a formal contract *early next month*.

我們希望下個月初正式簽約。

** ————————————————

look over 查閱　　president 〔'prɛzədənt〕 *n.* 董事長；總經理

訂 貨
基礎會話

UNIT 1

Ordering goods
有關訂貨

<**對話精華**>

- *We've decided to* order from you.
  我們已經決定向你們訂貨。

- We'll send our *official order* today.
  我們今天會寄上正式的訂單。

- *Did you get our order for* your copying machines?
  您是否有收到我們訂影印機的訂單？

❋ 催促買方訂貨 ❋

☺ Have you discussed whether you will order from us?

你們是否已討論過要不要向我們訂購？

☺ We haven't received an order from you. When are you going to decide?

我們還沒接到你們的訂單，你們何時可決定呢？

☺ *Our stock has run low.* I hope you'll order from us as soon as possible.

我們的存貨快沒了，我希望你們儘快訂貨。

**

order〔'ɔrdɚ〕*n.* 訂購；訂貨；訂單　　　run〔rʌn〕*v.* 成為；變為

℧ *Unless* you order in February, we *won't* be able to deliver in April.　除非您二月訂貨，否則我們無法四月送貨。

✳ 訂貨 ✳

℧ We'd like to order your products.　我們想訂你們的貨。

℧ We've decided to order from you.　我們已經決定向你們訂貨。

℧ We want to order your products.　我們要訂你們的貨。

℧ We'll send a trial order.　我們會寄上試驗訂單。

℧ We'll send our *official order* today.　我們今天會寄上正式的訂單。

℧ If we're satisfied with the first order, we'll order from you again.　如果我們滿意第一次訂的貨，我們會再向你們訂。

℧ *Did you get our order for* your copying machines?　您是否有收到我們訂影印機的訂單？

℧ Thank you very much for ordering from us. We've arranged *delivery*.　謝謝您向我們訂貨，我們已安排送貨了。

---

trial〔'traɪəl〕*adj.* 試驗的　　delivery〔dɪ'lɪvərɪ〕*n.* 交付；遞送

UNIT 2

About the stocks
有關存貨

<對話精華>

- We'd like to order a KM-36. Do you have that *on hand*? 我們想訂 KM-36，你們有現貨嗎？

- I'm sorry *we've got no inventory on that* at this time. 很抱歉，那個我們目前沒有存貨。

- We have *a large stock of* the goods.
  這貨品我們有很多的存貨。

☺ Do you have KM-36s *in stock*? 您有沒有 KM-36s 的庫存呢？

☺ We'd like to order a KM-36. Do you have that *on hand*? 我們想訂 KM-36，你們有現貨嗎？

☺ I'll have that information by tomorrow. 明天之前我會有消息。

☺ Will you wait while I see if we have them in stock? 我看看那些有沒有存貨時，請你等一等好嗎？

☺ I'm sorry, we're sold out of the goods at the moment. 很抱歉，現在貨已經賣完了。

℃ Thank you for your inquiry, but the goods are now ***out of stock***. I'm sorry. 　　謝謝您的查詢，可是現在沒存貨了，很抱歉。

℃ I'm sorry ***we've got no inventory on that*** at this time. 　　很抱歉，那個我們目前沒有存貨。

℃ We have only five of the items in stock. 　　那產品我們只有五台存貨。

℃ We have ***a large stock of*** the goods. 　　這貨品我們有很多的存貨。

**

out of stock 沒貨了

inventory〔'ɪnvən,torɪ〕*n.* 庫存品；清單

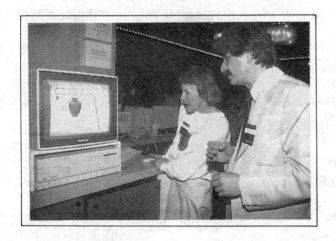

UNIT 3

Imports & exports
有關進出貨

<對話精華>

- When will you get a new *supply*? 你們何時要進貨？
- After ordering, *how long does it take* for delivery? 訂購之後，要多久才能送貨？
- They're *due to arrive in* Seattle on the seventeenth of April. 貨預定在四月十七日，送達西雅圖。

❀ **進貨日期** ❀

☺ When will you get a new *supply*?	你們何時要進貨？
☺ Please let us know immediately when we can have a new supply.	我們有貨可進時，請立刻通知我們。
☺ *We expect it to come in* around March fifteenth.	我們希望三月十五日左右進貨。
☺ We expect thirty to come in before the end of the month.	我們希望月底之前，能進貨三十台。
☺ Can you get it for us by next Wednesday?	下禮拜三前，您能替我們取得貨物嗎？

ଓ You'll have it by the end of next week *without fail*.

下週結束前，您一定拿得到。

✳ 出貨日期 ✳

ଓ Would you tell us your earliest delivery date？

您能告訴我們，你們最早的送貨日期嗎？

ଓ When will you be able to deliver？

你們何時能送貨？

ଓ When will the delivery be possible？

什麼時候可能送貨？

ଓ After ordering, *how long does it take* for delivery？

訂購之後，要多久才能送貨？

ଓ Delivery takes two months after we receive your order.

在接獲訂單後，要兩個月才能送貨。

ଓ The delivery date will be around the middle of September.

送貨日期在九月中旬左右。

ଓ Now, we're very busy, so I'm afraid it'll be about four months before we'll be able to deliver.

現在我們很忙，所以，恐怕大約四個月後，才能送貨。

ଓ We'll be able to deliver in two weeks.

我們兩週內便能送貨。

ଓ We can guarantee delivery before October tenth.

十月十日前，我們保證可以送貨。

♋ We'd like you to deliver by October (the) fifth.	我們希望你們十月五日前送貨。

※ 確認出貨日期 ※

♋ What is *the dispatch date* for the ES-37 we ordered last week?	我們上週所訂 ES-37 的發送日期是幾號?
♋ Would you confirm the order dispatch date?	您能確定一下發貨的日期嗎?
♋ I'd like reconfirmation of the dispatch date on those ES-37s we ordered a month ago.	我想再確定一下,我們一個月前所訂那些ES-37的發送日期。
♋ Could you reconfirm the shipping date for me?	您能替我再確定一下運送日期嗎?
♋ What's your order number?	您的訂單號碼是多少?
♋ They'll be sent next week.	下週會送去。
♋ They'll be sent on the fifth of March.	三月五日會送去。
♋ *They're scheduled* to be sent on March (the) fifth.	貨預定在三月五日送去。

---

dispatch〔dɪ'spætʃ〕*n.* 發送;速辦

℘ They'll be sent the day after
tomorrow and will arrive in
Seattle on the tenth of October.

後天會送貨,並於十月十
日抵達西雅圖。

℘ *They were shipped on* February
(the) tenth.

貨是在二月十日裝船的。

℘ They're *due to arrive in* Seattle
on the seventeenth of April.

貨預定在四月十七日,送
達西雅圖。

℘ They should arrive in Seattle
on the seventeenth of April.

貨應該在四月十七日送達
西雅圖。

UNIT 4

Changing an order
更改訂單

<對話精華>

- I have one change to *make* in the order.
  我想改一下訂單。

- We want to *substitute* KM-36 *for* KM-78.
  我們想以 KM-36，代替 KM-78。

- *We've complied with* your request for a change in your order.
  我們已順從您的要求，更改了訂單。

- I'd like to change my order. 我想更改訂單。

- I have one change to *make* in the order. 我想改一下訂單。

- Can we make a change on order No. 27903? 我們可以改一下第二七九○三號的訂單嗎？

- I'll check to see if they're loaded. 我查看看貨是否已裝載好了。

- I'm afraid they've been sent already. 恐怕貨已經送走了。

- I'm afraid it's too late. 恐怕太遲了。

☺ What kind of change do you have in mind?　　您想做怎麼樣的更改呢?

☺ What kind of change do you want to make?　　您要怎樣更改?

☺ We want to increase the number of EC-78s on order No. 27903.　　我們想增加二七九〇三號訂單上，EC-78的數量。

☺ We want to *substitute* KM-36 *for* KM-78.　　我們想以KM-36，代替 KM-78。

☺ I'll *look into* this and do the best I can.　　我會查查看，並且盡我所能。

☺ *We've complied with* your request for a change in your order.　　我們已順從您的要求，更改了訂單。

**

substitute A *for* B　以A代替B　　*look into* 調查
comply 〔kəm'plaɪ〕v. 順從；同意；應允

UNIT 5

Recommending another product
推薦另一種產品

<對話精華>

· There has been a model change. 款式改變了。

· We can *recommend* this brand as a good substitute.
我們可以介紹這種品牌，以爲替代。

ಟ I'm sorry it's not made. | 很抱歉，那沒有生產。

ಟ It's *no longer in production* and has been replaced by our new model. | 那已不再生產，並爲我們新型的產品所取代。

ಟ We changed the model. | 我們換了款式。

ಟ We *altered* the model. | 我們換了款式。

ಟ There has been a model change. | 款式改變了。

ಟ Can't you *take* the new model? | 您不能訂購新款式嗎？

ಟ We can *recommend* this brand as a good substitute. | 我們可以介紹這種品牌，以爲替代。

ಟ *We'll give you a* three percent *discount*. | 我們給您打九七折。

處理抱怨・索賠
基礎會話

CHAPTER IX

UNIT 1

Handling a complaint on undelivered goods
貨物未收到的抱怨及其處理

<對話精華>

- Would you wait three *more* days? 您能再多等三天嗎？

- The shipment *is stuck* in customs.
  出貨在海關遭到阻止。

- The shipment *has been delayed* because of a port
  strike. 出貨因港口罷工耽擱了。

❈ 未收到貨物 ❈

♤ Your shipment hasn't arrived yet. 　　　　　　你們載的貨還沒到。

♤ The *merchandise* ordered on September fifth hasn't arrived yet. 　　　　九月五日訂的商品還沒到。

♤ If we can't get them by September tenth, we'll have to *cancel* the order. 　　如果九月十日前無法拿到的話，我們就得取消訂貨。

**

shipment〔'ʃɪpmənt〕*n.* 裝船；出貨；所載之貨
merchandise〔'mɜtʃən,daɪz〕*n.* 商品

❀ 處理貨物未收到的抱怨 ❀

◊ I can't understand it. 　　　　我不明白。

◊ We will check into it and call 　我們會調查，並會盡快給
you as soon as possible. 　　您電話。

◊ That was shipped on September 　貨物是在九月十日運送的，
tenth. It should *reach* you in 　您應該兩、三天後會收到。
two or three days.

◊ Would you wait three more 　　您能再多等三天嗎？
days?

◊ The shipment *is stuck* in cus- 　出貨在海關遭到阻止。
toms.

◊ The shipment *has been delayed* 　出貨因港口罷工耽擱了。
because of a port strike.

◊ We're sorry for this delay. 　　這次的耽擱，我們很抱歉。

＊＊──────────────────────

stick〔stɪk〕*v*. 阻止；困住（*pp*. stuck）
delay〔dɪˈle〕*v*. 耽擱；延緩　　　strike〔straɪk〕*n*. 罷工

〰〰〰〰〰〰〰學英文的書，學習都有〰〰〰〰〰〰〰

UNIT 2

貨物受損、錯誤、
不足的抱怨及其處理

＜對話精華＞

· The goods were damaged in *transit*.
　貨物在運送途中受損了。

· The goods have been damaged by water, so they are
　beyond use. 貨物因受海水的損壞,所以不能用了。

· We sent the wrong articles *by mistake*.
　我們誤送了錯誤的商品。

❀ 貨物受損 ❀

◇ I'd like to explain about the damaged goods. 　　我想說明一下受損的貨物。

◇ The goods were damaged *in transit*. 　　貨物在運送途中受損了。

◇ How much was damaged? 　　有多少受損?

◇ About ten percent was damaged *on arrival*. 　　送達時,大約有百分之十的貨)受損。

**

damage〔'dæmɪdʒ〕*v.* 損壞　　transit〔'trænsɪt〕*n.* 運送;搬運

♤ Some of the goods are ***badly*** damaged. | 有些貨品嚴重受損。

♤ We're afraid half of the goods are damaged. | 恐怕有半數的貨受損了。

♤ I'm sorry, but all of the goods are damaged. | 很抱歉，所有的貨都受損了。

♤ The goods have been damaged by water, so they are ***beyond use***. | 貨物因受海水的損壞，所以不能用了。

♤ Everything is stained. | 全部都汙損了。

♤ The packing was not complete. | 包裝並不完全。

♤ We asked for a double-carton, but it came in a single-carton. | 我們要求用雙層的紙板盒，送達時卻是單層的紙板盒。

❈ 收到錯誤的貨物 ❈

♠ The goods we received are not what we ordered. | 我們收到的貨品，並非我們所訂購的。

♤ We didn't receive what we ordered. | 我們收到的不是我們所訂購的（貨品）。

♠ We ordered KM-32, but we received KM-22. | 我們訂的是KM-32，卻收到KM-22。

---

stain〔sten〕*v.* 汙損　　carton〔'kɑrtn̩〕*n.* 紙板盒

♤ The goods we received were different from the original sample.　我們所收到的貨品，與原樣品不符。

※ 收到的貨物數量不足 ※

♤ I'd like to explain about the shortage of goods.　我想說明一下，貨物不足的原因。

♤ We checked and found a short-age.　我們查驗時，發現了（貨物）不足。

♤ How many are you short?　你們缺了多少？

♤ We are short three units.　我們缺了三台。

♤ We ordered forty-five units and received only forty.　我們訂了四十五台，只收到四十台。

♤ The invoice *shows* forty-five units, but we received only forty.　發票上寫的是四十五台，但我們只收到四十台。

※ 處理貨物受損、錯誤及不足的抱怨 ※

♤ We'll send a representative to check the exent of the damage.　我們會派個代表，去檢查受損的程度。

---

shortage 〔'ʃɔrtɪdʒ〕*n.* 缺乏；不足　　　extent 〔ɪk'stɛnt〕*n.* 程度

♤ What shall we do with the damaged goods?

我們該如何處理受損品？

♤ Could you please **send** the damaged goods **back** to us?

您能將受損品，送還我們嗎？

♤ We will send you a credit for
the damaged goods.

我們會將受損品的信用貸款，寄給你們。

♤ We're sorry. We will send you
the correct product immediately.

很抱歉。我們會立刻送去正確的產品。

♤ We sent the wrong articles **by
mistake**.

我們誤送了錯誤的商品。

♤ We'll send a credit for what
we didn't deliver.

我們會送去，我們沒送的貨物的信用貸款。

＊＊

article〔ˈɑrtɪkḷ〕n. 物品

UNIT 3

Handling complaint on inferior goods

收到劣等品的抱怨及其處理

<對話精華>

- The goods you sent us are inferior *compared to* the original sample. 送來的貨比原樣品差。
- We found the goods inferior. 我們發現貨品很差。
- The goods are not *up to par*. 這些貨品未達標準。

※ 收到劣等品 ※

♤ The goods you sent us are inferior *compared to* the original sample.　　送來的貨比原樣品差。

♤ We found the goods inferior.　　我們發現貨品很差。

♤ The goods we received this time are inferior to those you sent when we placed our first order.　　我們這次收到的貨品，比初次訂購所送來的貨品差。

♤ The goods are not *up to par*.　　這些貨品未達標準。

♤ They don't work properly.　　它們不能正常運作。

**

inferior〔ɪnˈfɪrɪə〕*adj.* 次等的；較劣的
up to 及得上；到某一程度或部份　　par〔pɑr〕*n.* 標準

♤ It's obvious that you sent us defective articles.

顯然地，你們送來的是有瑕疵的貨品。

❋ 處理對貨物品質不滿的抱怨 ❋

♠ We admit the quality was not quite up to our usual standard.

我們承認，這次品質未達我們一般的標準。

♤ Would you send back the defective articles at our expense?

您能將缺損貨品,用我們公司的費用，寄回給我們嗎?

♤ If the goods are not what you expected, we'll be glad to exchange them.

如果貨品不是你們所期望的,我們很樂意更換。

＊＊

defective 〔dɪˈfɛktɪv〕 *adj.* 有缺點的；不完美的

UNIT 4

Handling mistakes on bills
票據的錯誤及其處理

＜對話精華＞

- The price on the invoice is different from *that* on the price list. 發票上的價格，與價目表上的不符。

- We'll send you our *revised* bill.
  我們會將改過的帳單，寄去給您。

- Please *destroy* our incorrect *statement*.
  請將我們錯誤的對帳單銷毀。

※ 票據上的錯誤 ※

♤ We received your invoice, but there was no discount.　　我們收到了貴公司的發票，可是却沒折扣。

♤ The discount rate is different from the contract.　　折扣率與合約不符。

♤ The contract *says* a thirty percent discount, but they've discounted only twenty percent.　　合約上說是打七折，不過却只打了八折。

＊＊

contract〔'kɑntrækt〕*n.* 合同；合約

♤ The price on the invoice is
different from *that* on the
price list.

發票上的價格，與價目表上
的不符。

♤ The invoice lists items we
didn't order.

發票上列了我們沒訂購的品
目。

♤ We received your *statement*,
but you charged us for items
we didn't order.

我們收到了貴公司的對帳單，
可是，我們沒訂的品目，貴
公司卻向我們索費。

♤ Last week I told you that
your invoice was wrong, but
you haven't sent me a correct
one yet.

上週我告訴您，您的發票有
誤，但是您還沒寄來正確的
發票。

※ 對於票據錯誤的處理 ※

♤ We're extremely sorry. We
will send you a correct invoice immediately.

非常抱歉。我們會將正確的
發票，立刻寄去給您。

♤ We'll send you our revised
bill.

我們會將改過的帳單，寄去
給您。

♤ Please *destroy* our incorrect
statement.

請將我們錯誤的對帳單銷毀。

**

price list 價目表　　item〔'aɪtəm〕*n.* 項目；品目
statement〔'stetmənt〕*n.* （商業上之）計算表；（支付）報告書，在此作
「對帳單」解

UNIT 5

Claim
索賠

<對話精華>

- Let's **arbitrate** the matter. 我們請人來仲裁這事兒。
- We'll **compensate for** the loss. 我們會補償損失。
- **We're filing a claim** with our insurance company.
  我們將向保險公司提出索賠。

※ 洽談賠償問題 ※

♤ We'll send **a claim note**.

我們將寄出一份索賠函。

♤ We think you should be responsible for the loss incurred **due to** the delay in delivery.

我們認爲貴公司應該負責因延遲運送所蒙受的損失。

♤ Our company is not responsible for that.

那個本公司是不予以負責的。

♤ We have a clear-cut **case** against the shipping company.

我們對船公司提出的訴訟，非但有理,而且有把握勝訴。

**────────────

claim〔klem〕*n.*〔商〕索賠　　note〔not〕*n.* 短簡；通告
incur〔ɪn'kɝ〕*v.* 蒙受（損失）
clear-cut〔'klɪr'kʌt〕*adj.* 清晰的；明確的

♤ We cannot accept your claim. 我們無法接受你們的索賠。

♤ We're sorry we can't **honor** your claim. 抱歉，我們無法接受你們的索賠。

♤ The matter seems to be **too** difficult for us **to** settle between us. 這件事情，似乎很難由我們雙方來解決。

♤ Let's **arbitrate** the matter. 我們請人來仲裁這事兒。

♤ Please **compensate for** the loss we suffered because of the poor quality of your goods. 請賠償我們因你們公司產品品質低劣，所蒙受的損失。

♤ The question is the **amount of compensation**. 問題在於賠償額是多少。

♤ We'll give you an additional discount of ten percent on this shipment. 我們對於這次的貨品，會給您額外打九折。

♤ We'll give you a discount on the repair. 修理方面，我們會給你們打折。

♤ We'll compensate for the loss. 我們會賠償損失。

---

honor〔'ɑnɚ〕v. 接受之而到期付款
arbitrate〔'ɑrbə,tret〕v. 仲裁；公斷
compensate〔'kɑmpən,set〕v. 賠償；償還
suffer〔'sʌfɚ〕v. 蒙受；遭受

✳ 關於保險公司的賠償 ✳

♤ We asked the insurance adjuster to come out and investigate.

我們要求保險理賠人來作調查。

♤ We'll contact our insurance company.

我們將連絡我們的保險公司。

♤ Does the insurance company pay *full value* for damage?

保險公司對於損壞的，會作全額的賠償嗎？

♤ Will full compensation be made?

會全部賠償嗎？

♤ We're fully insured.

我們受到全額的賠償。

♤ They say they can't compensate for the damage.

他們說他們無法補償損失。

♤ They say the fault *lies in* your use of the product.

他們說，問題出於您對產品的使用。

♤ *We're filing a claim with* our insurance company.

我們將向保險公司提出索賠。

＊＊─────────────

adjuster 〔ə'dʒʌstə〕*n.* 調停者；〔保險〕理賠人
investigate 〔ɪn'vɛstə,get〕*v.* 調查；研究
file 〔faɪl〕*v.* 提出（訴訟）

UNIT 6

Payment
付　款

<對話精華>

- The ***deadline for settlement*** is April (the) tenth.
  結清期限是四月十日。

- We've remitted ten thousand dollars to you ***through***
  the bank. 我們已透過銀行，滙給您一萬（美）元。

- We're looking forward to your remittance.
  我們正等著您的滙款。

✻ 希望買方儘快寄來信用狀 ✻

♤ We have not received the ***letter
of credit*** yet.　　　　　　　　我們尚未收到信用狀。

♠ Would you send a letter of
credit covering your order?　　　請寄來涵蓋您訂貨的信用狀
　　　　　　　　　　　　　　　好嗎？

♤ Without your letter of credit
we can't ***negotiate*** your ***bills***.　沒有信用狀，我們無法給貴
　　　　　　　　　　　　　　　公司押滙。

♤ We'd like you to open a letter
of credit as soon as possible.　　我們希望您儘快開信用狀。

---

negotiate〔nɪ'goʃɪ,et〕v. 轉讓；押滙；使（支票、證券等）流通

❋ 對要求開具信用狀的答覆 ❋

♤ We opened a letter of credit today.

我們今天開了信用狀。

♤ The letter of credit was mailed to you yesterday.

信用狀於昨天寄給您了。

♤ We think the letter of credit will **reach** you by April tenth.

我們想，信用狀在四月十日前會寄達給您。

♤ We're very sorry for the delay in opening the letter of credit.

我們很抱歉遲開信用狀。

❋ 請求付款 ❋

♤ We'll send you a **statement of your credit**.

我們會寄給您一份對帳單。

♤ Would you send us a check to **settle the balance**?

您能寄一張支票來結清尾款嗎？

♤ Would you send your check by April tenth?

您能在四月十日前，把支票寄來嗎？

♤ The **deadline for settlement** is April (the) tenth.

結清期限是四月十日。

---

deadline〔ˈdɛd͵laɪn〕*n.* 截止日期   settlement〔ˈsɛt!mənt〕*n.* 清算

◇ We're looking forward to your remittance.

我們正等著您的滙款。

※ 通知賣方支票已開 ※

◇ We've sent our check for $14,530.

我們已寄出一萬四千五百三十（美）元的支票。

◇ We've remitted ten thousand dollars to you *through* the bank.

我們已透過銀行，滙給您一萬（美）元。

◇ We've sent our check for $10,000 *in partial payment* of your invoice of October (the) fifth.

您十月五日開的發票，我們已寄出部份款項一萬（美）元。

◇ We've arranged payment of your invoice.

您的發票，我們已安排好付款。

**

remittance〔rɪ'mɪtn̩s〕*n.* 滙寄之款；滙款

UNIT 7

Handling complaint on protesting late payments

抗議未付款的抱怨及其處理

<對話精華>

· Your account is *long overdue*. 你的帳單已逾期很久了。

· May we have a three week *extension* of payment？
  我們可以延長三個星期付款嗎？

· We'll *settle* our *account* within two weeks.
  我們兩週內會償清帳目。

❋ 抗議未付款 ❋

♤ We haven't received your remittance yet.

我們尚未收到你的滙款。

♤ Your account is *long overdue*.

你的帳單已逾期很久了。

♤ Your account is already two
  months overdue.

你的帳單已逾期兩個月了。

♤ We can't wait any longer.

我們不能再等了。

♤ Please pay within seven days.

請在七天內付款。

**

account〔ə'kaʊnt〕*n.* 帳目；帳單
overdue〔'ovə'dju〕*adj.* 過期的；逾期的

♧ If we don't receive your payment within seven days, we'll
hand the account **to** our law-
yer.

如果七天內我們沒收到付款，
我們將會把帳單交給我們律
師。

※ 處理未付款的抱怨 ※

♧ May we have a three week
extension of payment?

我們可延後三個星期付款嗎?

♧ We'll be able to pay **before
long**.

我們不久就可以付款。

♧ We'll **settle** our account within two weeks.

我們兩週內會償清帳目。

**—————————————————

before long 不久

Vocabulary Street　信用狀專用術語

☐ negotiable letter of credit 可轉讓信用狀

☐ non-negotiable letter of credit 不可轉讓信用狀

☐ revocable letter of credit 可撤銷信用狀

☐ irrevocable letter of credit 不可撤銷信用狀

☐ confirmed letter of credit 保兌信用狀

☐ unconfirmed letter of credit 不保兌信用狀

~~~~~~~~~~~~~~~~~~~~~~~~~~~~~~~

☐ sight letter of credit 即期信用狀

☐ time letter of credit 遠期信用狀

☐ L/C with red clause 紅條款信用狀

☐ traveler's（negotiable）letter of credit 旅行（流動）信用狀

☐ commercial letter of credit 商業信用狀

☐ back-to-back letter of credit 憑轉信用狀

☐ reimbursement letter of credit 還款信用狀

☐ revolving letter of credit 循環信用狀

☐ stand-by letter of credit 備用信用狀

~~~~~~~~~~~~~~~~~~~~~~~~~~~~~~~

☐ paying bank 付款銀行　　bank of acceptance 承兌銀行

☐ confirming bank 保兌銀行　　advising bank 通知銀行

☐ issuing（open）bank 開（發）狀銀行

☐ negotiating bank 押滙銀行

商業交易
實況會話

UNIT 1

Negotiation
商 議

<對話精華>

· Can I come and see you now？ 我現在可以過去見你嗎？
· **_Am I calling at a bad time_**？
    我這通電話是不是打得不是時候呢？
· I'll arrange my schedule to **_fit_** yours.
    我會安排我的時間來配合你。

※ **約談**(1) ※

A : Hello. This is Chen. Are you busy now？

A：喂，我姓陳，請問你現在忙嗎？

B : Oh, hello, Mr. Chen. Not really. Why？

B：哦，嗨，陳先生。我不很忙，有事嗎？

A : **_Can I come and see you now_**？ I got to see you right away.

A：我現在可以過去見你嗎？我得立刻見你。

B : OK, but what seems to be the problem？

B：好的，不過是不是有什麼問題？

A : Can I tell you when I see you in person？

A：我見到你本人時，再告訴你好嗎？

B : All right.

B：好的。

❋ 約談(2) ❋

A : Hello ! May I speak to Mr. Jones, please ?

A : 喂！我可以找瓊斯先生聽電話嗎？

B : This is he.

B : 我就是。

A : Oh, how are you ? This is Mr. Chen of the Henry Trading calling.

A : 噢，你好嗎？我是恒利貿易公司的陳先生。

B : Oh, I see. What can I do for you ?

B : 噢，我知道了。有什麼我能爲你效勞的嗎？

A : I hope *I'm not calling at a bad time*.

A : 希望我這通電話不會打得不是時候。

B : No, no ! Not at all.

B : 不，一點也不會。

A : It just came to my mind that we should get together tomorrow morning and talk over the deal I mentioned this afternoon.

A : 我剛剛有個念頭就是，我們明天早上應該碰個面，討論一下我今天下午提起的交易。

B : That's fine. What time shall we meet ?

B : 好呀，我們什麼時候碰面？

**

talk over 討論　　deal〔dil〕*n.*（俗）交易

✻ 應允約談 ✻

A : Hello, is this Mr. Jackson from Chicago?

A : 喂，你是來自芝加哥的傑克森先生嗎？

B : Yes, I am.

B : 是的，我是。

A : This is Mr. Chen of the Henry Trading Company.

A : 我是恒利貿易公司的陳先生。

B : Oh, yes. As a matter of fact, I was about to get in touch with you. Mr. Ford told me a lot about you and asked me to look you up as soon as I got here.

B : 噢，是啊。事實上，我正要和你聯絡。福特先生告訴我很多有關你的事，並且要我一到這兒就來拜訪你。

A : Is that right?

A : 是嗎？

B : What time shall we meet?

B : 我們什麼時候見面？

A : Well, *I'll arrange my schedule to fit yours*. So, just tell me what time is convenient for you.

A : 唔，我會安排我的時間來配合你。因此，你只要告訴我你什麼時候方便。

✻ 約定會面時間 ✻

A : What time shall I come?

A : 我幾點可以過去？

B : Any time after two is alright with me.

B : 兩點以後的任何時間，我都可以。

A : Fine. ***I'll come and get you
　　at three***. Where will you
　　be then?

A：好，我三點過來接你，
　　你那時候會在哪裏？

B : I'll be down in the lobby.

B：我會在樓下的大廳。

A : O.K. I'll see you then.

A：好的，到時候見。

B : All right. I'm looking forward
　　to meeting you.

B：好的，我期待見到你。

※ 表示暫時抽不開身(1) ※

A : May I speak to Mr. Hung,
　　please?

A：我可以請洪先生聽電話
　　嗎？

B : This is he. Who is this,
　　please?

B：我就是，請問是哪位？

A : Oh, how are you? This is
　　Mr. Sanders from Houston.

A：哦，你好嗎？我是從休
　　士頓來的山度士。

B : Gee, when did you arrive in
　　Taiwan?

B：噫！你什麼時候到台灣
　　的？

A : I just got in an hour ago.
　　Can I see you this afternoon?

A：我才剛到一個小時。今
　　天下午能見你嗎？

B : Well…***I'm all booked up today***.
　　How about catching me to-
　　morrow?

B：嗯，…我今天一點兒都
　　沒空。明天找我怎麼樣？

---

lobby〔ˈlɑbɪ〕*n.* 大廳　　***look forward to*** 盼望；期待
get in 到達　　***booked up*** 〔話〕一點兒都沒空

✻ 表示暫時抽不開身(2) ✻

A : Can I see you sometime this week ?

B : *I'm afraid I'm fully booked this week*, but I can make it sometime next week.

A : Good.

A：這禮拜的哪個時候，我可以見你嗎？

B：恐怕我這禮拜都很忙，不過下禮拜我可以撥個空。

A：好。

✻ 安排參觀工廠 ✻

A : Would you be able to make a quick trip to our Kaohsiung plant next Monday ?

B : I am not quite sure if I can make it. I'm supposed to have a lunch with an American friend of mine on Monday.

A : Well, in that case, *let's make it tentatively for Monday*.

B : That's good.

A：你可以儘快在下週一來我們高雄廠嗎？

B：我不太確定是否可以。週一我應該和一位美國朋友共進午餐。

A：唔，若是那樣的話，讓我們暫定是星期一好了。

B：好。

**

plant〔plænt〕*n.* 工廠　　*be supposed to* 應該
in that case 若是那樣的話　　tentatively〔'tɛntətɪvlɪ〕*adv.* 暫時地

❋ 約時間再談 ❋

A : We must meet again to discuss this sometime next week.

A : 我們必須下個禮拜，再找
個時間討論此事。

B : O.K. *When can you make it* ?

B : 好啊！你什麼時候可以？

A : How about Friday afternoon ?

A : 星期五下午怎麼樣？

B : That suits me perfectly.

B : 那完全適合我。

A : Good. Can you come over
again ?

A : 好極了,你可以再過來嗎？

B : No problem.

B : 沒問題。

❋ 約定以後再談 ❋

A : What are some of the problems we may face ?

A : 我們可能會面臨一些什麼
樣的問題？

B : Well, as for tariffs we found
out that our products would
not be liable for duty.

B : 嗯，至於關稅，我們發現
我們的產品並不需要繳稅。

A : What about shipping facilities?

A : 船運設備如何呢？

----

come over 從遠處來；訪問　　　*as for* 至於
tariff〔ˈtærɪf〕*n.* 關稅表；關稅
liable〔ˈlaɪəbl̩〕*adj.* 有義務的；有責任的
duty〔ˈdjutɪ〕*n.* 關稅　　　facility〔fəˈsɪlətɪ〕*n.* 設備（常用 *pl.* ）

B : That can be a problem. There are only a very few direct sailings. Well, *I'm afraid there isn't much time left for further discussion today.* So may I suggest we discuss it again at the next meeting?

B：那可能是個問題。直達的航線很少。唔，今天恐怕沒剩多少時間，做更進一步的討論了。因此，我建議下次見面時，我們再討論好嗎？

❊ 約會遲到 ❊

A : Hey, you're late! You are supposed to be here at 3 p.m.

A：嘿，你遲到了！你應該（下午）三點到的。

B : Please forgive me. I was so darn busy *I almost forgot our appointment.*

B：請原諒我。我實在是忙得差點忘了我們的約會。

A : Well, that happens, but I almost gave up on you, you know.

A：唔，這種事總會發生的。只是你可知道，我差一點就不等你了。

❊ 逾時未到 ❊

A : Don't tell me you're already leaving!

A：別告訴我你準備要走了！

B : Well, I have a 7 o'clock appointment and I guess I'd better be going.

B：唔，我七點鐘有個約會，我想我最好現在就走。

** forgive〔fəˈgɪv〕*v*. 原諒　　darn〔dɑrn〕*adv*. 非常地

A : But, my boss *is due here any minute* now, and he is so anxious to meet you.

A : 可是，我老闆隨時會到，他極渴望見到你。

B : Well, in that case, I'll stick around a few more minutes.

B : 唔，若是那樣的話，我就再多等幾分鐘好了。

**

due〔dju〕*adj*. 應到的　　*anxious to* 渴望
stick around〔俚〕在附近逗留或等待

UNIT 2

Inquiries
詢　問

~~~~~~ ＜對話精華＞ ~~~~~~

· How about ***giving me a rundown on it***?
  口述大要給我聽一下如何？

· What's ***the total amount of*** your annual sales?
  貴公司的年總銷售額是多少呢？

· What's your ***market share***? 貴公司的市場佔有率是多少？

※ 詢問市場狀況⑴ ※

A: How is the market situation
   in your country?

A：貴國的市場狀況如何？

B: Well, it is so-so, not too
   bright, not too dark, I should
   say.

B：唔，馬馬虎虎啦，我應
   該說不很好,也不很壞。

A: ***Give me a tip-off*** if anything
   drastic should happens there,
   OK?

A：萬一有什麼激烈的事發
   生,給我個密報好嗎？

B: Sure, any time.

B：當然，隨時會通知你。

**

tip-off〔'tɪp,ɔf〕*n.*（賽馬或投機事業中的）密報；警告；暗示
drastic〔'dræstɪk〕*adj.* 激烈的；猛烈的

❋ 詢問市場狀況⑵ ❋

A： You come to Taiwan quite
often, don't you?

B： Well, I drop by in Taipei
whenever I take a trip around
the countries in Southeast
Asia.

A： Then you must be quite familiar with the garment markets in that part of the world.
*How about giving me a rundown
on it*?

B： With pleasure.

A：你來台灣來得十分勤，
不是嗎？

B：唔，每當我到東南亞各
國旅行時，都會順便到
台北。

A：那你一定對該地區的服
裝市場相當熟悉了。口
述大要給我聽一下如何？

B：我很樂意。

❋ 詢問市場狀況⑶ ❋

A： Mr. Smith, thank you for all
the information you've given
me.

B： Any time.

A： Oh, by the way, I have one
more question.

A：史密斯先生，謝謝你提
供我的所有資料。

B：（有問題）隨時歡迎你來。

A：噢，對了，我還有一個
問題。

**————————————————

Southeast Asia 東南亞　　garment〔ˈgɑrmənt〕*n.* 服裝
rundown〔ˈrʌn,daʊn, ˈrʌnˈdaʊn〕*n.* 概要（報告）；口述大要

B : *Shoot* !

B：開始說吧！

A : Do you have any idea how steel markets are going in Europe nowadays?

A：你知不知道，目前歐洲的鋼鐵市場狀況如何？

※ 市場調查(1) ※

A : Well, I'm a little hazy about your question. How much is the national income per capita — *is that what you are asking*?

A：嗯，我有點弄不清你的問題。每人每年的國民所得是多少──你是這樣問的嗎？

B : No, it's not. What I'd like to ask is if it has been rising in this country lately or not?

B：不，不是這樣。我想問的是，該國國民的年所得近來是否有增加？

A : I see. May I draw your attention to this chart? Here, obviously it's rising very fast.

A：我懂了。可以請你注意一下這圖表嗎？瞧這兒，很明顯地它增加得非常快。

---

shoot 〔 ʃut 〕 *v*.〔俗〕開始講話
hazy 〔'hezɪ〕 *adj*. 不清的；模糊的
national income （每年度的）國民所得
capita 〔'kæpɪtə〕 *n*. 頭；人（ *pl*. of caput）   chart 〔 tʃɑrt 〕 *n*. 圖表

❋ 市場調查(2) ❋

A : May I ask you just one more question, Mr. Barkley?

A：巴克力先生，我可以再多請教您一個問題嗎？

B : Sure. Go right ahead.

B：當然可以。問吧！

A : Do you think our products are competitive enough in an international market?

A：您認爲我們的產品，在國際市場上經得起競爭嗎？

B : Pricewise yes, but in terms of its guaranteed service over a long period of time, I would say no.

B：就物價來講，可以的。但以長期保證服務的觀點來看，我就要說不行了。

A : I'll keep that in my mind. Well, *thank you very much for sparing so much of your precious time.*

A：我會記住您所說的。非常謝謝您撥出這麼多寶貴的時間。

B : That's all right. Any time.

B：別客氣。歡迎隨時再來。

❋ 採購探詢 ❋

A : Hello. Shinpoong Trading Company. May I help you?

A：喂，新鵬貿易公司。我能幫您什麼忙嗎？

---

competitive〔kəm'pɛtətɪv〕*adj.* 競爭的；經得起競爭的
pricewise〔'praɪs͵waɪz〕*adv.* 就物價而論　　*in terms of* 以～之觀點
spare〔spɛr〕*v.* 撥出（時間）

B : Yes. I'm in town to buy a substantial quantity of coffee mugs. And someone asked me to get in touch with you.

B : 是的，我到城裏來，是 爲了探購大量的咖啡杯。 有人要我和你聯絡。

A : Thank you very much for calling. *We'll be happy to come over and discuss the matter anytime you suggest*. Who's calling, please?

A : 非常感謝您打電話來， 我們很樂意在任何您方 便的時候前去拜訪，並 和您討論此事。請問貴 姓大名？

B : Mr. Taylor of the Samuelson Co. of Los Angeles. I'm now staying at Lotte Hotel, Room 212.

B : 我是洛杉磯山姆森公司 的泰勒先生，現在住在 樂得飯店，二一二號房。

❋ 詢問產品種類 ❋

A : Besides musical instruments, what else do you produce?

A : 除了樂器，你們還生產 什麼？

B : Well, we manufacture furniture, motorbikes, skis and other sporting goods.

B : 唔，我們生產傢俱、機 動腳踏車、雪橇和其他 的運動用品。

*
---

substantial〔səb'stænʃəl〕*adj.* 大量的
mug〔mʌg〕*n.* 圓筒狀有柄的大杯子　　**get in touch with** 和～聯絡
musical instrument 樂器　　furniture〔'fɜnɪtʃə〕*n.* 傢俱
motorbike〔'motə,baɪk〕*n.* 機器腳踏車（＝*motorcycle*）
ski〔ski〕*n.* 雪橇　　goods〔gʊdz〕*n.pl.* 物品；貨物

A : ***What are your main products***
among those？

A：其中什麼是你們的主產
品？

B : They used to be motorbikes,
but now skis and other sporting goods are replacing them.
I would put skis at the top
of the list.

B：過去是機動腳踏車，但
如今被雪橇和其它的運
動用品取代了。我把雪
橇列為是最主要的產品。

❋ 詢問產量 ❋

A : Do you have overseas plants
as well？

A：你們也有國外廠嗎？

B : Yes, we have one in America
and two in Thailand. We're
building another in Mexico.

B：是的，美國有一家，泰
國有兩家。現在要在墨
西哥另建一家。

A : ***What's your monthly produc-***
tion capacity for this model？

A：貴公司這個型的每月的
產量是多少？

B : This one is manufactured only
for the domestic market, so
let me see... it would be
approximately fifty thousand.

B：這一型僅製造供應國內
市場，因此讓我想想看
…大約是五萬吧。

---

overseas〔'ovɚ'siz〕*adj.* 海外的；國外的　　*as well* 也；亦
Thailand〔'taɪlənd〕*n.* 泰國　　capacity〔kə'pæsətɪ〕*n.* 能力；容量
manufacture〔,mænjə'fæktʃɚ〕*v.* 製造

※ 詢問業績 ※

A: What's the percentage of overseas markets in proportion to domestic markets for your products?

B: The ratio is about 7 overseas to 3 domestic.

A: I see. *What's the total amount of your annual sales*?

B: For the fiscal year 1987 it was a little over 900 million dollars.

A: 貴公司產品，國內外市場的比例是多少？

B: 大概是國外七對國內三之比。

A: 我知道了。貴公司的年總銷售額是多少呢？

B: 就一九八七會計年度而言，稍稍超過九億美元。

※ 詢問貨品銷售力 ※

A: I understand you are one of the largest manufacturers of optical goods in this country. Could I ask a bit more about sales figures?

B: Sure. Go right ahead.

A: 我知道貴公司是本國最大的光學用品廠商之一，我可以再多問一些有關銷售額的事嗎？

B: 當然，請問吧。

---

in proportion to 與…成比例 ratio 〔'reʃo〕 n. 比例
annual 〔'ænjʊəl〕 adj. 每年的 fiscal 〔'fɪskḷ〕 adj. 財政的；會計的
manufacturer 〔͵mænjə'fæktʃərə〕 n. （大規模的）廠商
optical 〔'ɑptɪkḷ〕 adj. 光學的

A： *What's your market share?*　　A：貴公司的市場佔有率是
　　　　　　　　　　　　　　　　　　多少？

B： If I'm not mistaken, it was　　B：如果我沒搞錯，去年超
　　　over 85 percent last year.　　　過了百分之八十五。

❋ 詢問自己產品的銷售情形 ❋

A： How has our latest model　　A：我們最新款式的銷售情
　　　been accepted?　　　　　　　　形如何？

B： It's been very well accepted.　B：好極了。而舊款式的需
　　　There's still a great demand　　求量也依然很大。
　　　for your old model, too.

A： Oh, why?　　　　　　　　　　A：噢，爲什麼？

B： Because the price is reason-　B：因爲價格合理，且容易
　　　able and it's easy to carry.　　携帶。

A： You mean it's small enough　A：你是指它夠小，而適合
　　　to fit into a pocket?　　　　　放進口袋裏嗎？

B： That's right.　　　　　　　　B：對的。

❋ 回答詢問 ❋

A： Hey, where is Mr. Chen?　　A：嘿，陳先生在哪裏？

＊＊

　market share 市場佔有率　　demand〔dɪ'mænd〕*n.* 需要；需求
　fit into 適合

B : Which Mr. Chen do you mean? We have about two dozen Mr. Chens, you know.

A : I'm talking about the tall, lanky guy who used to handle European exports.

B : Oh, you mean our section chief? He's stepped out for a few minutes.

A : Isn't he going to get a transfer to one of your overseas branches?

B : *Not that I know of.*

B : 你指的是哪個陳先生？你可知道，我們有大約兩打的陳先生。

A : 我說的是高高瘦瘦，向來是處理歐洲出口的那個。

B : 噢，你是說我們組長？他已出去好幾分鐘了。

A : 他不是即將調到你們其中一個國外分公司嗎？

B : 我聽說不是。

---

lanky〔ˋlæŋkɪ〕*adj.* 瘦長的　　transfer〔ˋtrænsfɚ〕*n.* 調任
branch〔ˋbræntʃ〕*n.* 分行；分店
know of (or *about*) 懂得；知道；聽說

UNIT 3

Sales
推銷

<對話精華>

· I'll give you a **super deal**. 我會給你一個特價。

· Do you follow me？ 你聽得懂我說的嗎？

· Give it to us **straight**. 你直接告訴我們。

❋ 提供選擇式推銷 ❋

A：We have here two kinds of hanging planters. Which do you prefer？

A：我們這兒有兩種懸掛式的盆栽。你比較喜歡哪一種？

B：Well, I guess **either will do**, but if you insist that I make a choice, I will take this one with the fancy cord.

B：嗯，我想哪一種都可以。但是如果你堅持要我作個選擇，我會選帶有華麗細繩的那一種。

A：All right. Actually we're getting more orders for that one because of its luxurious decoration.

A：好的。事實上，我們接到愈來愈多那種樣式的訂單，因爲它有華麗的裝飾。

**

either will do 隨便哪一個都行 insist〔ɪnˋsɪst〕v. 堅持；強調
cord〔kɔrd〕n. 細繩；索 luxurious〔lʌgˋʒʊrɪəs, lʌkˋʃʊrɪəs〕adj. 華麗的

❋ 展示推銷 ❋

A : May I help you ?

B : Yes. Could you show me how to operate this machine ?

A : Certainly. Put the tape on and press this button.

B : Oh, I see. How simple !

A : *Can I interest you in this new model* ? This is even simpler than that one. It's fully automatic.

A：我可以爲您效勞嗎？

B：是的。你可以教我操作這台機器嗎？

A：當然可以。把錄音帶放上去，按下這個鈕。

B：噢。我懂了。多簡單啊！

A：您對這新機型有興趣嗎？這甚至比那種更簡單，是全自動的。

❋ 推銷新產品(1) ❋

A : Here is our latest model. I want you to take a close look at the exquisite design !

B : Ummm… It looks pretty enough. How much are you asking for this ?

A : Well, *you name it*.

A：這兒是我們最新的款式。希望你仔細看看這精美的設計！

B：呃…看起來相當漂亮。這個你們要價多少？

A：嗯，你出個價吧。

---

operate〔'ɑpə,ret〕*v*. 操作；運轉　automatic〔,ɔtə'mætɪk〕*adj*. 自動的
take a look at 看…(一眼)；看一看
exquisite〔'ɛkskwɪzɪt, ɪk'skwɪzɪt〕*adj*. 精美的
design〔dɪ'zaɪn〕*n*. 設計；圖樣

B : It's hard for me to make an offer simply because I'm not familiar with the markets.

B : 我很難出價，因為我對市場並不熟悉。

✻ 推銷新產品(2) ✻

A : This is our latest model of the portable translation machine we've been discussing.

A : 這是我們討論過的最新型的手提傳譯機。

B : Oh, it's so compact !

B : 噢，好小巧！

A : Yes, it's small enough to fit into a pocket.

A : 是啊，小到可適於放進口袋。

B : How much is it ?

B : 這多少錢？

A : *I'll give you a super deal.*

A : 我會給你一個特價。

✻ 介紹產品 ✻

A : This product of ours is carefully designed to insure full satisfaction to its users. *Do you follow me ?*

A : 我們這項產品，是為了確保其使用者能完全滿意，而精心設計的。你聽得懂我說的嗎？

---

make an offer 出價　　portable〔'pɔrtəbḷ,'pɔrtəbḷ〕*adj.* 手提的
compact〔kəm'pækt〕*adj.* 小巧的
super〔'supɚ,'sjupɚ〕*adj.* 〔俚〕特等的；特佳的
insure〔ɪn'ʃʊr〕*v.* 確保　　satisfaction〔,sætɪs'fækʃən〕*n.* 滿意
follow〔'falo〕*n.* 聽得懂（說明等）

B : Sure I do.

A : Good. I thought my English was somewhat insufficient to make you fully understand what I meant to say.

B : No, no! I understand you perfectly.

B : 當然聽得懂。

A : 好。我想，要讓你完全了解我所說的，我的英文是稍嫌有些不夠。

B : 不，不會！我完全了解你說的。

❋ 單刀直入式垂詢(1) ❋

A : Mr. Johnson, would you give us your frank opinion about our products and their prices?

B : Well…I…am not so familiar with them in the first place…

A : Then, you think our prices are too steep?

B : Well, I didn't exactly say that! What I meant to say is that…

A : 強森先生，對於我們的產品與價格，你能給我們你的意見嗎？

B : 嗯…我…首先我對它們並不很熟…

A : 那你覺得我們的價格不太合理嗎？

B : 呃，我不完全是那個意思！我的意思是…

---

in the first place 早先；首先
steep〔stip〕*adj.* 不合理的；過分的
not exactly 不完全是；未必

A : Oh, come on, Mr. Johnson.
Give it to us straight. Are
you going to buy our products?

A：噢，強森先生，請別這
樣。你直接告訴我們，
你會買我們的產品嗎？

❋ 單刀直入式垂詢⑵ ❋

A : What do you say to the idea
that we put this deal to bed
once and for all ?

A：讓我們徹底地做成這個
交易，你覺得怎麼樣？

B : I wish I could do so.

B：我希望我可以這麼做。

A : What do you mean by that ?
You are not sure about this
whole deal ?

A：你這麼說是什麼意思？
你對這整樁交易，仍不
確定嗎？

B : *I had only half a mind* to buy
this product in the first
place.

B：首先，我只有一點點意
思想買這個產品。

A : Well, well…then it's a different story now.

A：唔…，那麼現在完全不
是那麼一回事囉。

＊＊

come on 請（常用懇求語氣）　　*once and for all* 堅決地；最終地
have half a mind ～有幾分想～
a very different story 完全不同的一回事

UNIT 4

Price negotiations
議　價

> **＜對話精華＞**
>
> ・ Oh, *don't try to rip me off*！噢！別想騙我！
> ・ *You can say that again*！你說的一點兒也沒錯。
> ・ May I ask what you are getting at？
> 　我可以請問你指的是什麼嗎？

✳ 殺價 ✳

A : How much would you ask for this coffee set ?

B : Well, ordinarily it's \$12.30! But since our business relationship is of long standing, I will make it \$10.40.

A : Oh, *don't try to rip me off*! I can get the same stuff at \$9.20 easily.

A：這套咖啡組，你要價多少？

B：唔，一般是要十二元三毛美金！不過考慮到我們長久以來的貿易關係，我算你美金十元四毛。

A：噢，別想騙我！我可以輕易地以九元兩毛美金，買到相同的東西。

---

rip *sb.* **off** 欺騙（某人）　　stuff〔stʌf〕*n.* 物品；事物

❋ 抗議對方報價不一 ❋

A : Hey, what kind of talk is
that ? Only a minute ago,
you said this is $2.70, and
now you are saying that...

A : 喂，那是什麼話？才一
分鐘以前，你說這個是
兩塊七毛美金，而你現
在却說…

B : Please wait a minute. What
I meant to say in the begin-
ning was...

B : 請等一下，我一開始說
的是…

A : Oh, knock it off ! You said
this is $2.70, right ?

A : 噢，不要吵！你說這是
兩塊七毛美金的,對吧?

B : *Please don't raise your voice!*

B : 請別提高嗓門！

A : OK, OK !

A : 好！好！

❋ 表示自己價錢漲得合理 ❋

A : How much are you asking for
a dozen of this?

A : 你這個一打要價多少？

B : The best price we can come
up with is $8.50.

B : 我們所能提供最合理的
價錢是八塊五毛美金。

A : Wow, the prices have gone up
sharply, haven't they ?

A : 哇，這價錢漲得眞快，
不是嗎？

---

knock it off 停止！不要吵！(通常用以喝止爭吵、打架或爭執)
come up with 提議；建議

B : *You can say that again*! The production cost alone has doubled in the past year.

B：你說的一點兒也沒錯！單單是製造成本，在去年一年裏，就增加爲兩倍了。

❈ 說明自己無法降價 ❈

A : I wonder if you can get them done somehow in a way that...

A：我想知道，你可不可以多多少少這樣子做…

B : *May I ask what you are getting at*?

B：我可以請問，你指的是什麼嗎？

A : Sure. All I want to know is if it's possible to expect any reduction on these prices.

A：當然可以。我想知道的是，這些價錢，可不可能降低一點。

B : I'm afraid it's not. These are really our bottom wholesale prices.

B：恐怕不能。這實在是我們的批發底價了。

A : I see.

A：我懂了。

B : Actually due to the current oil shortage, materials have gone up incredibly, you know.

B：事實上，由於目前石油短缺，物價漲得令人難以置信，你知道嗎？

⁂

get sth. down 完成某事　　*in a way* 多少；有幾分　　*get at* 意指；暗示
reduction〔rɪ'dʌkʃən〕*n.* 減低　　wholesale〔'hol,sel〕*adj.* 批發的
materials〔mə'tɪrɪəlz〕*n.pl.* 必需品；用具　　*go up* （價格）上漲
incredibly〔ɪn'krɛdəblɪ〕*adv.* 令人難以置信地

❋ 表示自己價錢很便宜 ❋

A : How much are these per dozen ?

A : 這些每打多少錢 ?

B : The regular market price runs as high as ＄5.90 per dozen. But ours are only ＄4.30 flat. *It will be a real steal*!

B : 一般市價高到每打五塊九毛美金，但是我們一律只賣美金四元三毛。這眞是便宜貨呀！

A : Well, I don't know about that. I must talk with my boss before I make up my mind.

A : 唔，我不懂那個。做決定之前，我必須和我老闆討論一下。

❋ 表示對方價錢殺得太離譜 ❋

A : What do you think of our price ?

A : 你認爲我們的價格如何 ?

B : Frankly speaking, I cannot approve your price !

B : 老實說，我無法同意你們的價格！

A : Why is that ?

A : 那是爲什麼 ?

B : Because I can buy the same thing in Japan at one third of your price.

B : 因爲我可以在日本，以你們價格的三分之一，買到相同的東西。

A : Oh, *that's a laugh*! I can't believe it !

A : 噢，開玩笑！我才不信！

---

market price 市價　　steal〔stil〕*n.*〔俗〕很便宜買到的東西

✻ 表示對方開價太高 ✻

A: How much would you want for this coffee mug?

A：這個咖啡杯要多少錢？

B: Well, it all depends on what pattern you decide to take.

B：嗯，那要看你決定要什麼樣式。

A: Suppose I take this windmill pattern?

A：如果我要這個風車形的呢？

B: Well, for that particular model, it will be $6.70 per dozen.

B：嗯，那種特殊樣式，每打要六塊七毛美金。

A: Oh, no! *Too steep*!

A：哇！不行！太貴了！

B: I don't think so. You must compare our price with those asked by other export houses.

B：我不這麼認為，你必須拿我們的價錢和其他出口商出的價錢相比。

---

mug〔mʌg〕*n.* 杯　　windmill〔'wɪnd,mɪl〕*n.* 風車
steep〔stip〕*adj.* 過分的；不合理的

UNIT 5

Signing contracts

簽 約

<對話精華>

・What's the **term** of this contract?
這契約的期限多長？

・Does what it say here mean that...
這裏說的是不是指…

・What are **the major channels of distribution** within
the country? 國內商品配銷的主要管道是什麼？

※ 確認合約期限 ※

A： Are there any other questions?

B： Just one more thing. **What's the term of this contract?**

A： As it says here, it's three years and upon its expiration it will be renewed every three years subject to agreement of both parties.

A： 有任何其他問題嗎？

B：只剩一個問題。這契約的期限多長？

A： 正如這裏所寫的，是三年期限，期滿時，會根據雙方的同意，每三年重訂一次。

**

expiration〔͵ɛkspəˋreʃən〕*n.* 期滿
subject to 依照；根據

renew〔rɪˋnju〕*v.* 更新；重訂

B： Does it mean then, one or the other can discontinue it every three years if there's a disagreement between the two?

B：那麼，它是說，如果雙方意見不合，任何一方，可以在三年期滿時中止契約？

A： That's right.

A：是的。

❋ 確認契約內容 ❋

A： Before we sign this contract, may I confirm a couple of things?

A：在我們簽約之前，我可以確定幾件事嗎？

B： Yes, of course. What are they?

B：當然，什麼事？

A： *Does what it say here mean that* residuals should be paid?

A：這裏說的是不是指應給付附加酬勞？

B： That's right.

B：是的。

A： Oh, I see.

A：噢，我知道了。

**

discontinue〔͵dɪskən'tɪnjʊ〕*v*. 中止；廢止
contract〔'kɑntrækt〕*n*. 合約；合同
confirm〔kən'fɝm〕*v*. 確定；證實
residual〔rɪ'zɪdʒʊəl〕*n*.（因重播而付給演員的）附加酬金

✳ 確認產品配銷管道 ✳

A： I'm more concerned with your domestic markets. ***What are the major channels of distribution*** within the country?

A：我比較關心你們國內的市場，國內商品配銷的主要管道是什麼？

B： We are totally on what we call a "chain store" system.

B：我們完全憑藉所謂的「連鎖店」制度。

A： You mean there's no wholesale process in-between?

A：你是說其中沒有批發的過程嗎？

B： That's correct.

B：對了。

✳ 確定對方完全了解合約內容 ✳

A： I'm going to dictate the terms of this contract to you.

A：我要口述這項合約的內容給你記錄下來。

B： O.K. Go ahead.

B：好呀，說吧。

＊＊

domestic〔dəˈmɛstɪk〕*adj.* 國內的　　channel〔ˈtʃænḷ〕*n.* 途徑
distribution〔͵dɪstrəˈbjuʃən〕*n.*（商品的）配銷
chain store 連鎖店　　in-between〔͵ɪnbɪˈtwin〕*adj.* 介乎中間的
dictate〔ˈdɪktet, dɪkˈtet〕*v.* 口述；口授令人筆錄

A : Once I finish the dictation, *will you read it back to me*? I want to confirm if I have conveyed them to you correctly. My English pronunciation is terrible, you know.

A：等我一唸完，你可以把它讀一遍給我聽嗎？我想確定一下，我是否正確地把意思傳達給你。我的英語發音很差，你是知道的。

B : No, I think your pronunciation is perfect.

B：不，我認為你的發音很好。

✳ 抱歉自己算錯金額 ✳

A : Here is the total amount of money involved in this contract.

A：這裏是有關這合約的全部金額。

B : Let me see... Say, I think you got this shipping charge all wrong. It's supposed to be $5,800 instead of $6,200.

B：我看看…喂，我想你（船）運費全算錯了。應該是五千八百美元，而不是六千兩百美元。

A : Gee, *I'm sorry, I blew it*! I got all mixed up with something else.

A：噫，對不起，我搞混了！我把這和其他的算在一起了。

B : That's all right. That can happen.

B：沒關係。這是很可能發生的。

**

convey〔kən've〕*v.* 傳達　　*mix up* 混合

UNIT 6

Demanding actions & reminders
催促及提醒

<對話精華>

- I'll get it to you *first thing in the morning*, O.K.?
  我（明天）一大早就把它拿來給你好嗎？

- Well, this one *is pressing*, but the other one can *wait*. 嗯，這個很緊迫，不過另一件可以緩一緩。

- *What's the rush*? 急什麼？

※ 催促對方在期限內做決定 ※

A: How soon can we expect your answer to our proposal?

A: 關於我們的提議，我們多久能得到你的答覆？

B: Well, I can't be sure now, because I have to check with my boss back at home.

B: 唔，我現在無法確定，因為我必須回去跟我老闆確定一下。

A: All right. Then I'll *give you until next Wednesday*, OK?

A: 好吧。那麼，我給你到下星期三的期限，好嗎？

B: I don't know. I also have to look up many things before I make up my mind.

B: 我不知道。在我做決定之前，我也必須查閱很多東西。

A： Well, then, we'll wait till
Saturday.

A：唔，那麼我們等到下星
期六。

B： That's fine. Saturday will
do.

B：那很好。星期六可以的。

❋ 提醒對方帶樣品 ❋

A： Have you brought the sample?

A：你把樣品帶來了嗎？

B： My god！ I forgot all about
it！

B：老天！我全忘了！

A： Please be sure to get me
one before I leave.

A：我離開之前，請務必給
我一個。

B： I'll get it to you *first thing
in the morning*, O.K.?

B：我（明天）一大早就把
它拿來給你，好嗎？

A： O.K.!

A：好！

❋ 催貨⑴ ❋

A： How soon would you like to
have them done?

A：你要我多久把這些做好？

B： Well, *this one is pressing,
but the other one can wait*.

B：嗯，這個很緊迫，不過
另一件可以緩一緩。

❋❋────────────────

the first thing in the morning 一大早

pressing〔'prɛsŋ〕*adj.* （事態等）緊迫的；火急的

A: When is this one due?

B: Tomorrow afternoon.

A: Oh, that's impossible.

B: I understand, but could you please squeeze it in somehow?

A：這個什麼時候要？

B：明天下午。

A：噢，那是不可能的。

B：我知道，不過，能不能請你想辦法把它趕出來？

❋ 催貨(2) ❋

A: We'd like to place an order for one thousand units of this component.

B: You mean catalogue No. 2158?

A: Yes. And we need them immediately. Could we get them delivered this afternoon?

B: Well, we wish we could, but...

A：我們想訂一千個這種零件。

B：你是指目錄上的二一五八號嗎？

A：是的，我們馬上就要。能不能今天下午就送過來給我們？

B：我們希望可以，不過…。

---

squeeze〔skwiz〕v. 搾；壓迫；〔話〕強迫；危急，在此有「趕一趕」的意思

somehow〔'sʌm,haʊ〕adv. 以某種方法

component〔kəm'ponənt〕n. 成份；構成要素，在此指「零件」

A: *I know it's difficult, but we'd appreciate if you could.* We're completely out of stock at present.

A：我知道這很難，但如果你們可以的話，我們會很感激的。我們目前完全缺貨。

❋ 催貨(3) ❋

A: How soon can you ship out the order? Would the shipment get to us in time for Christmas?

A：你們多久能出這批貨？這批貨能在聖誕節前，及時送到我們手中嗎？

B: Well, that I have to figure out.

B：嗯，那我要推算一下。

A: Come on! Let's get over with this deal for now!

A：別這樣啦！我們現在就這麼說定了吧！

B: *What's the rush?* "Haste makes waste," you know!

B：急什麼？你是知道的，「欲速則不達」！

A: That's true, but...

A：的確，但…

B: Please no more buts!

B：請別再說但是了！

---

appreciate 〔ə'priʃɪ,et〕v. 感激　　*out of stock* 缺貨
at present 目前；現在　　*ship out* 〔*off*〕（用船）把貨物裝出
figure out 把…算出　　*get over* 做完；完成
rush 〔rʌʃ〕v. 匆忙；急促
Haste makes waste. 欲速則不達；忙中有錯

※ 追踪訂單 ※

A: Hello. This is Mr. Jones of
Union Electronics Co., Ltd.
I'm calling in connection with
an order we placed a long
time ago.

A：喂，我是聯邦電子有限
公司的瓊斯先生。我是
打電話來問，關於我們
很久以前訂貨的事。

B: May I have the reference
number of your order, please?

B：請告訴我您訂單的號碼
好嗎？

A: Certainly. It's No. 1205/
FRS. It was made by tele-
phone on Aug. 15th and confirmed by a letter a week
later.

A：當然，號碼是 1205 /
FRS，是八月十五日以
電話訂，一個星期後以
信確定的。

B: Just a moment. Let me look
into it... Hello. Now I've
found out everything about it.
It's going to be a long story.

B：請等一下，讓我查查看
…，喂，現在我已查出
所有有關它的一切。真
是說來話長。

A: Oh? What kept it so long?

A：哦？是什麼使它說來話
長？

---

in connection with 關於；與…相關連
look into 翻查；調查　　*find out* 查出

Vocabulary Street 國際貿易專用術語

- □ export declaration 出口報關　certificate of export 出口簽證
- □ declaration for export 出口申報單 (= *E/D*)
- □ declaration for import 進口申報單
- □ import (export) license 輸入 (出) 許可證
- □ shipping advise 裝船通知單　freight note 運費請求書
- □ inquiry sheet 詢價單
- □ proforma invoice 估價單 (= *quotation*)
- □ letter of indemnity 賠償書；保險證書

- □ partial delivery 分批交貨　installment shipment 分批裝船
- □ place (time) of delivery 交貨地點 (時間)
- □ date of shipment 裝船日期
- □ shipping order 裝貨單 (*S/O*)
- □ delivery order 發貨單 (*D/O*)
- □ bill of lading 提單 (*B/L*)

- □ storage charge 倉庫費　packing charge 包裝費
- □ loading & discharging charge 裝卸費
- □ export subsidy 出口津貼　permit fee 簽證費
- □ extension fee 延期費　confirming charge 保兌費
- □ acceptance charge 承兌費　margin money 保證金

商場應對
實況會話

CHAPTER IX

1. 拜訪
2. 與客戶寒喧
3. 商談途中的談話
4. 邀請・招待・道別

UNIT 1

Visiting
拜 訪

＜對話精華＞

· Mr. Lin, something ***has come up*** that I have to talk
to you about. 林先生，發生事情了，我必須和你談一談。

· You came to the ***right*** person. 你找對人了。

· I couldn't possibly ***wait that long***.
我可能無法等那麼久。

※ **歡迎來訪** ※

A : It's nice of you to come.
Please have a seat, won't you?

B : Thank you.

A : Did you have any difficulty
finding our office?

B : No, I didn't. The map you
mailed helped me a lot.

A : Did it? Good! ***Would you
like a cup of Taiwanese oolong***?

A：你能來真好。請坐，好
嗎？

B：謝謝。

A：你找我們公司難不難？

B：不，不難。你寄給我的
地圖，幫了我很大的忙。

A：真的？那很好！你要不
要來一杯臺灣烏龍茶？

---

oolong〔ˈulɔŋ, ˈulɑŋ〕*n.* 烏龍茶

❋ 表明來訪的理由 ❋

A : May I help you ?

A : 我可以為您效勞嗎 ?

B : I'd like to see Mr. Lin. My name is Jack Chen.

B : 我想見林先生。我叫陳傑克。

A : Do you have an appointment ?

A : 您約過時間了嗎 ?

B : No, I don't, but I have some very important business to talk about.

B : 不 , 沒有 , 不過我有一些很重要的事要談 。

A : Just a moment. Mr. Lin, Mr. Chen wants to talk to you on the phone.

A : 請等一下 。林先生 , 陳先生要跟您講電話 。

B : Thank you. Mr. Lin, something has come up that *I have to talk to you about*.

B : 謝謝你 。林先生 , 發生事情了 , 我必須和你談一談 。

❋ 招呼訪客 ❋

A : May I help you ?

A : 我可以為你效勞嗎 ?

B : Yes, I'm looking for a Mr. Chang who is in charge of the export department.

B : 是的 , 我要找一位張先生 , 他是負責出口部門的 。

---

come up （問題等）發生　　*in charge of～*　負責照料

A : *You came to the right person.*
I'm Mr. Chang himself.

B : Oh, is that right？What a
surprise！

A：你找對人了。我就是張
先生本人。

B：噢，是嗎？多令人驚訝
啊！

❈ 過訪未遇 ❈

A : I'm here to see Mr. Roberts.

B : Mr. Roberts was suddenly
called away. He should return
soon, though.

A : How long will he be？

B : He should be back in an hour,
at the latest.

A : An hour！ *I couldn't possibly
wait that long.*

B : Would you care to schedule
another appointment？

A : Yes, let's do that.

A：我是來見羅伯茲先生的。

B：羅伯茲先生臨時有事出
去了。不過，他應該很
快就會回來。

A：他要出去多久？

B：最遲一個小時內應該會
回來。

A：一個小時！我可能無法
等那麼久。

B：你要不要另外定個時間
呢？

A：好吧，就這麼辦。

❋❋————————————————————

surprise〔 səˊpraɪz 〕*n.* 驚訝；驚奇
schedule〔ˊskɛdʒʊl 〕*v.* 排定：〔俗〕安排（某事）於將來某特定的日期

UNIT 2

Small talk with customers
與客戶寒喧

<對話精華>

· Well, *it varies* from company to company.
  嗯，各個公司不同。

· *You're pulling my leg.* 你在開我玩笑吧。

· I want to *hit the sack* early tonight.
  今晚我要早點睡。

❋ 閒談(1) ❋

A: How many hours a week do you work in Taiwan?

A：在臺灣，你們一週工作幾小時？

B: Well, *it varies from company to company.*

B：嗯，各個公司不同。

A: How about in your company?

A：你們公司怎樣？

B: We work forty-four hours a week. In some other companies forty hours, but not every week, every other week.

B：我們一週工作四十四小時。其它有些公司，並非每週，而是每隔一週，工作四十小時。

A: I see.

A：我懂了。

---

vary〔'vɛrɪ〕 v. 不同　　*every other* 每隔一（日，小時，週等）

❋ 閒談(2) ❋

A : Tell me. Why do you work
　　so hard?

B : Well, *we have to eat*, *you*
　　know.

A : I know, but earning your daily
　　bread is not everything in
　　life, is it?

B : Of course not. So I think I
　　should have more time for doing
　　something else, but in Taipei
　　that's easier said than done.

A : 告訴我。爲什麼你們這
　　麼拼命工作?

B : 唔,我們都得吃飯過活,
　　你知道的。

A : 我知道啊,但是餬口並
　　不是生活的全部,不是
　　嗎?

B : 當然不是囉!所以,我
　　想我應該有更多的時間
　　做別的事,只是在台北
　　說比做更容易。

❋ 閒談(3) ❋

A : Hello. How are you?

B : Fine, thank you. And you?

A : Oh, I'm O.K., too.

B : I suppose you are busy as usual.

A : Yes, I am. *There's no rest for*
　　the wicked, *you know*. How
　　about you?

A : 喂。你好嗎?

B : 好,謝謝。你呢?

A : 噢,我也很好。

B : 我想你像往常一樣忙。

A : 是啊!邪惡的人總是沒
　　辦法休息,你是知道的。
　　那你呢?

---

as usual 像平常;照例
wicked〔ˈwɪkɪd〕*adj.* 邪惡的;不道德的;〔謔〕惡作劇的;淘氣的

B : I'm also busy running from one job to another.

B：我也一樣爲一個個的工作奔忙。

A : I understand. Life in Taipei is a rat race.

A：我了解。台北的生活競爭得很激烈。

❈ 問問客戶投宿的情形 ❈

A : How is the hotel you're staying at now? Have you found it comfortable?

A：你現在住的這家旅館怎樣？你覺得舒服嗎？

B : Not only comfortable, you can get all the excitements of the night life right there.

B：豈止是舒服，在那兒你可以享盡夜生活中的種種刺激。

A : Is that right?

A：是嗎？

B : Yes, I really lived it up last night. I'd never enjoyed so much in my life.

B：是的，昨晚我眞的狂歡了一夜。我一生中，從未這麼快樂過。

A : *You're pulling my leg.*

A：你在開我玩笑吧。

B : No, honest! That's true!

B：不，實在話。是眞的！

❈ 閒談經貿 ❈

A : How is business in Taiwan lately?

A：近來臺灣的貿易情形如何？

**

rat race 激烈競爭　　*live it up* 享受人生；過快樂的日子
pull a person's leg 開（某人的）玩笑

B: Not so good, I'm afraid. *Sales have been down greatly these days.*

B：恐怕不很好。近來銷售額大幅減少。

A: Have they? The same in America.

A：是這樣嗎？美國也是。

B: It's due to the current inflation caused by the shortage of oil.

B：這是由於石油短缺，引起目前通貨膨脹之故。

A: You said it.

A：我完全同意。

※ 閒談出口業 ※

A: The export business seems to be soaring these days, doesn't it?

A：出口業最近似乎頗爲景氣，不是嗎？

B: Yes, it does. I think it's good. That'll greatly help improve our economy, won't it?

B：是的，的確。我想這是好現象。那對我們的經濟改善，會有很大的幫助，不是嗎？

A: *Well, I don't know about that.* Things don't seem to be quite that simple.

A：嗯，這個我不知道。事情似乎沒有那麼簡單。

B: What do you mean?

B：你的意思是什麼？

**
be down 減少　　*these days* 目前	inflation〔ɪnˈfleʃən〕*n.* 通貨膨脹
shortage〔ˈʃɔrtɪdʒ〕*n.* 缺乏；不足	soar〔sor〕*v.* 升騰；升高

❀ 閒談公司狀況 ❀

A : How is your company doing
　　these days?

A : 你們公司最近進展得如
　　何?

B : *Just between the two of us,*
　　we are far ahead of our export
　　target.

B : 這可是我們之間的秘密,
　　我們已遠超過我們的出
　　口目標了。

A : Is that right?

A : 是嗎?

B : Yes, if things go as they do
　　now, I think we'd be able to
　　double our yearly objective
　　by the end of the year.

B : 是的,如果事情照現在
　　的情況進展的話,我想
　　在年底以前,我們就能
　　達到年目標的兩倍了。

A : You don't say!

A : 不可能吧!

❀ 談到其他公司⑴ ❀

A : Incidentally Jones Co., Ltd.
　　is getting stronger and stronger
　　in overseas markets.

A : 讓我順便提一下,瓊斯
　　有限公司的海外市場愈
　　來愈強了。

B : Yes, it is, and we're happy to
　　see it growing.

B : 是的,的確。我們很高
　　興見到它成長。

A : *How is your company affiliated*
　　with it?

A : 你們公司和那家公司有
　　何關係?

**

between the two of us 我們之間的秘密　　target〔'tɑrgɪt〕*n.*(生產等的)目標
incidentally〔ˌɪnsə'dɛntl̩ɪ〕*adv.* 順便一提地
affiliate〔ə'fɪlɪˌet〕*v.* 使有密切關係

B： It's one of our subsidiary companies.

B：它是我們附屬的公司之一。

A： Oh, I see. We can't beat them for their incrediblv low market prices.

A：噢，我明白了。我們無法打敗他們，因為他們的市場價格，低得令人難以置信。

❋ 談到其他公司⑵ ❋

A： Say, have you heard what has become of the S. Group?

A：喂，你聽說S集團遭遇什麼事沒有？

B： No！What has happened？

B：沒有！怎麼了？

A： The entire group has gone bankrupt.

A：整個集團都破產了。

B： *That really surprises me*.

B：那真的令我很訝異。

❋ 談正事前的寒喧 ❋

A： Long time no see. How have you been？

A：好久不見了。近來如何？

B： OK. I guess. How was the flight from the States？

B：我想還好啦。你從美國來的這趟飛行感覺如何？

----

subsidiary〔səb'sɪdɪˌɛrɪ〕 *adj*. 附屬的
incredibly〔ɪn'krɛdəblɪ〕 *adv*. 難以置信地
become of 使遭遇　　bankrupt〔'bæŋkrʌpt〕 *adj*. 破產的

A： Excellent！Smooth as silk, as they say. By the way, how is your family? Last time I was here, one of your kids was in some sort of traffic accident.

A：好極了！如他們所說的，像絲般的平穩。對了，你的家人好嗎？上回我在這兒時，你一個孩子好像出了什麼交通意外。

B： He's okay now. Well, ***shall we get down to business***?

B：他現在好了。唔，我們要不要靜下心來談事情了？

A： Good.

A：好啊。

❋ 談判後的閒聊 ❋

A： How about going out for a drink or two? We have had such a tiring day.

A：出去喝一、兩杯如何？我們已經辛苦一天了。

B： No, I don't think so. ***I want to hit the sack early tonight***.

B：不，我不這麼認為。今晚我要早點睡。

A： Are you sure?

A：你確定？

B： I'm positive. I will probably sleep like a rock after what we've been through today.

B：我確定。經過這樣一天之後，我可能會睡得很熟。

**

by the way 順便提起
get down to（*one's work*）靜下心（工作）
tiring〔'taɪərɪŋ〕*adj.* 辛苦的；麻煩的；令人疲倦的
hit the sack 就寢

UNIT 3

Small talk during business negotiation
商談途中的談話

＜對話精華＞

- Gee, *you're talking over my head*.
  噫，你的話我不懂。

- Let's *call it a day*. 我們就到此為止。

- We sell those only *by the set*. 我們只賣整組。

※ 表示聽不懂對方的話 ※

A : Since our country is experiencing a recession of considerable dimension at this moment, we cannot possibly bring ourselves to execute a purchase which is quite beyond our means.

B : Gee, *you're talking over my head*.

A：因為我們國家，此刻正面臨相當大規模的經濟蕭條，所以我們不可能購買超過我們財力所及的物品。

B：噫，你的話我不懂。

**

recession 〔rɪ'sɛʃən〕 *n.* 蕭條　　dimension 〔də'mɛnʃən〕 *n.* 規模；範圍
execute 〔'ɛksɪ,kjut〕 *v.* 執行；實施；完成
talk over one's head 講超過某人能了解的話

A : Am I?

B : Yes, I can't follow you very
well. Would you mind using
simpler words?

A : Of course.

B : Thank you.

A : 是嗎?

B : 是的,我聽不太懂你說
的。你介不介意用較簡
單的話?

A : 當然可以。

B : 謝謝。

❈ 談判毫無進展 ❈

A : We've been talking over this
deal for the past seven hours
and we don't seem to be getting anywhere!

B : That's true. I'm sort of
tired after all this talking.

A : *Let's call it a day* and go
out for some drinks!

B : That's a superb idea. After
all, I'm so hungry that I can
eat a horse.

A : 我們討論這筆生意已經
七個鐘頭了,但是似乎
毫無進展。

B : 的確。經過這討論後,
我有點累了。

A : 我們就到此為止,出去
喝幾杯吧!

B : 這主意真好。畢竟我餓
得可以吃掉一匹馬了。

---

talk over 討論　　deal〔dil〕*n.* 交易
get anywhere 成功;有效　　***call it a day*** 到此為止;暫時停止
superb〔su'pɜb, sə'pɜb〕*adj.* 極好的

❋ 同意暫停談判 ❋

A： Oh, come on, let's cut out this tiring process of business for now and go out to grab a bite.

A：噢，讓我們現在停止這辛苦累人的過程，出去找些東西吃吧。

B： But we have to put this business to rest today, remember?

B：但我們今天必須把這件事告一段落的，記得嗎？

A： I know, I know. But I'm starving.

A：我知道，我知道。可是我餓死了。

B： OK! I'll give up. *Have it your way*! We'll all go out and eat! How does that sound?

B：好吧！我投降。隨你便！我們全都出去吃吧！怎麼樣？

A： Great!

A：太棒了！

❋ 叫醒發呆的對方 ❋

A： Hey, wake up! *A penny for your thoughts*!

A：嘿，清醒！呆呆地想些什麼！

---

cut out 停止
starve 〔starv〕 *v*. 飢餓；渴望　　*have one's way* 隨心所欲
a penny for your thoughts 呆想

B : Oh, nothing much. I am just tired after all this talking, I guess.

B：哦，沒什麼。我想我只是經過這討論後，覺得累了。

A : I imagine you are. But we got to get this over with, you know.

A：我想你是。但是我們必須完成此事，你是知道的。

B : You're right. Let's get back to business.

B：你說的對。讓我們回到正事吧。

❈ 說錯話即時修正 ❈

A : Mr. Chen, how soon can we expect to have your shipment reach our destination?

A：陳先生，你們的貨何時可以送達我們的目的地？

B : It will get there not later than the end of April.

B：四月底之前將會送達。

A : Are you sure you can get it out so quickly? If I understand correctly, it takes more than a month and a half just to have the products readied for shipment.

A：你確定能這麼快嗎？如果我知道的沒錯的話，光是準備產品的裝船，就得花超過一個半月的時間。

❈❈────────────────────

get over 結束；完成

destination〔͵dɛstə'neʃən〕 *n.* 目的地

B : Gee, that was a slip of the tongue. *I take that back*. I forgot all about the time factor involved with the production.

A : I figured so.

B : 噫，那是一時失言，我收回那句話。我完全忘了要把製造的時間算進去。

A : 我想也是。

❋ 與老闆磋商 ❋

A : How long is the lease?

B : Five years.

A : 租期多長？

B : 五年。

A : Would it be possible to rent it on a shorter lease?

B : I think it would. But *let me have a word with my boss first*. May I use the phone?

A : Sure. Go ahead. And will you ask if the rent is still negotiable or not?

A : 租期能不能短一點？

B : 我想是可以，不過，讓我先和我的老闆聯絡一下，我能用電話嗎？

A : 當然，請便。請你問問他，租金是否還能再磋商，好嗎？

---

slip of tongue 說溜了嘴；一時失言　　*take back* 收回
involve 〔 ɪnˈvɑlv 〕 v. 包括；影響　　figure 〔ˈfɪgjɚ, ˈfɪgə 〕 v. 想；認為
lease 〔 lis 〕 n. 租期　　*have a word with* 與～說一兩句話
negotiable 〔 nɪˈgoʃɪəbḷ 〕 adj. 可磋商的

❋ 表示不能接受對方的條件 ❋

A : How do you like this coffee set?

A：你喜歡這咖啡組嗎？

B : Well, they look attractive enough to me. But don't you break up the set? I only want to buy this creamer.

B：嗯，它們看起來很吸引我。不過，你們不可以拆賣這組用具嗎？我只想買這個裝乳酪的小瓶。

A : I'm sorry, but we don't break up the set. *We sell those only by the set.*

A：抱歉，我們不拆賣這組用具，我們只賣整組。

B : Well, in that case, let's see... I'll take 300 sets on a trial.

B：嗯，那樣的話，我想想看…我就拿三百組試用看看。

---

break up 分開　　creamer〔'krimɚ〕*n.* 裝乳酪的小瓶
on trial 試用；暫時

UNIT 4

Invitations, entertaining & saying good-bye
邀請 · 招待 · 道別

～～～ ＜對話精華＞ ～～～

- Shall we drop in somewhere for a couple of drinks？
  我們要不要順便找個地方喝幾杯？
- I'll **pick up the tab**. 我來付帳。
- Here's a little something for you. 這兒有樣小東西送你。

※ 談判後邀飲 ※

A： Do you have anything to do
   after this？

B： No, I don't.

A： **Shall we drop in somewhere**
   for a couple of drinks？

B： That sounds like a good idea.

A： I know a very interesting
   place.

B： Oh, do you？ Good.

A：這個之後，你還有什麼
   要做的嗎？

B：不，沒有了。

A：我們要不要順便找個地
   方喝幾杯？

B：這主意聽起來不錯。

A：我知道一個很有趣的地
   方。

B：噢，你知道？太好了！

**

drop in 順便拜訪；順便到
a couple of ～ 兩（但美國人俗用亦作「數個」或「幾個」解）

❈ 談判後招待客戶遊逛 ❈

A：It's been a long and tiring
negotiation.

B：Yes. But I'm glad we've at
last put a finishing touch
to it.

A：So am I. How about having
a drink or two to celebrate
the successful conclusion of
our business？

B：That sounds good. But,
instead, care for looking
around the city？ After all
the weather is too beautiful
to stay indoors.

A：That's an excellent idea！

B：Good, *I'll show you around
the city*.

A：眞是一場冗長而令人疲
倦的談判。

B：是啊。不過我很高興我
們終於談完了。

A：我也是。爲了慶祝這項
生意圓滿談成，我們去
喝幾杯怎麼樣？

B：這主意聽起來不錯。不
過，要不要換成四處看
看這城市？畢竟天氣好
得不該待在屋子裏。

A：眞是好主意！

B：好極了，我帶你四處看
看這個城市。

❈ 招待咖啡 ❈

A：Say, you forgot your coffee.
It's getting cold.

A：嘿，你忘了你的咖啡了。
它漸漸快冷掉了。

---

negotiation〔nɪ,goʃɪ'eʃən〕*n.* 談判　　*care for* 喜歡；意欲

B : I'm afraid it's cold already.　B：恐怕已經冷了。

A : Do you want me to get you another cup of coffee?　A：要不要我給你另一杯咖啡？

B : No, no！ That's all right. I don't mind drinking cold coffee.　B：不，不用了！沒關係。我不介意喝冷咖啡。

※ 招待用餐 ※

A : Well, it's been a delicious meal.　A：嗯，這實在是豐盛美味的一餐。

B : Yes, this restaurant happens to be one of the best in town.　B：是啊，這家餐館正好是市內最好的幾家之一。

A : Is that right? Now, shall we get on our way?　A：是嗎？現在，我們是不是該走了？

B : Yes. And *I'll pick up the tab.*　B：好的。我來付帳。

A : Thank you for the lunch.　A：謝謝你招待這頓午餐。

B : Oh, think nothing of it. It's been a pleasure.　B：啊，這沒什麼，那是我的榮幸。

---

get on one's way 往目的地　　*pick up the tab* 支付～之費用
think nothing of 認為無所謂

❋ 招待飲酒 ❋

A： Phew！I think I had one too many.

A：啐！我想我喝太多了。

B： Oh, no！We've killed only half a dozen bottles of beer altogether.

B：噢，不會！我們總共才喝完半打啤酒。

A： Is that all？Anyhow, let's blow this joint. The air is getting rather too thick.

A：就這樣嗎？不管怎樣，我們走了吧！氣氛愈來愈讓人受不了了。

B： OK！*It's on me.*

B：好吧！我請客。

A： Thanks.

A：謝謝。

❋ 極力邀請客戶出外共餐 ❋

A： I want to invite you and Mr. Thompson out before I leave.

A：在我離開之前，我想邀請你和湯普森先生出外共餐。

B： That isn't necessary at all.

B：這倒不需要。

A： No. *I really want to do it.*

A：不。我是衷心邀請的。

---

phew〔fju, pfju〕*interj.* 呸！啐！（表示憎厭、不耐、驚訝等之聲）
kill〔kɪl〕*v.* 用完；完全消耗　　thick〔θɪk〕*adj.*〔俗〕不能忍受的
on〔ɑn〕*prep.* 表示動作或影響之直接或間接的接受（如 It's on me 表示
　「由我付帳」，也就是「我請客」的意思。）

B : In that case, we'll be glad
to go along.

B：既然如此，我們樂意一
起去。

❋ 婉拒邀遊 ❋

A : Are you free next weekend ?

A：你下週末有空嗎？

B : I'm afraid I'm not. I'm
going on a fishing trip.

B：恐怕沒有。我要去釣魚。

A : Oh, really！ I just thought
it might be fun to visit one
of those nightclubs.

A：喔，真的！我只是想，去
夜總會可能會很好玩。

B : I wish I could join you.

B：真希望能和你一起去。

A : Oh, that's O.K. *Let's make*
it some other time.

A：噢，沒關係，我們找其
它時間去。

❋ 邀請對方到辦公室坐坐 ❋

A : Are you still with K & C,
Co., Ltd. ?

A：你仍然在 K & C 股份有
限公司嗎？

B : Yes, I am. Why ?

B：是啊，為什麼你會這樣問？

A : I called your office the other
day, and the man who answered
the phone said there was no
such person here.

A：前幾天，我打電話到你
公司，接電話的人說，
這裏沒這個人。

** ────────────────────

along〔ə'lɔŋ〕*adv*. 共同

B : That's probably because I've been transferred. *I'm in the sales department* and my office is in an annex. Please drop by when you can come out this way.

B : 這很可能是因爲我調職了。我現在在銷售部門，而我的辦公室是在一間別館裏。你要是有到這裏來，請進來坐一坐。

※ 道別 ※

A : What time are you leaving ?

A : 你什麼時候走？

B : I'm supposed to get to the airport before 7 o'clock.

B : 我應該七點以前到機場。

A : Well, I won't be able to make it to the airport to see you off.

A : 唔，我無法到機場爲你送行。

B : Oh, that's all right. I know how to get around.

B : 噢，沒關係。我知道怎麼走。

A : *I'll miss you very much.*

A : 我會非常想念你。

B : I'll miss you, too.

B : 我也一樣會想你。

---

transfer〔træns'fɝ〕 v. 調職　　annex〔'ænɛks〕 n. 附屬建築物；別館
drop by（短暫或未經計畫的）拜訪
see sb. off 給某人送行　　*get around* 到處走動

❋ 道別贈禮 ❋

A : When are you heading back home ?

A：你何時動身回家？

B : I'm supposed to get on the plane tomorrow evening.

B：我應該明天晚上上飛機。

A : Well, it's been a pleasure to work with you.

A：唔，跟你一起工作，是件愉快的事。

B : I feel the same way.

B：我有同樣的感覺。

A : *Here's a little something for you.*

A：這兒有樣小東西送你。

B : Oh, how nice of you ! May I open it ?

B：噢，你真好！我可以打開嗎？

A : By all means. I hope you'll like it.

A：當然可以。希望你會喜歡。

✳✳

by all means 當然；必定

公司業務
實況會話

CHAPTER XII

UNIT 1

Inside the office
公司內部

＜對話精華＞

- Now let me *get down to the main business*.
  現在讓我言歸正傳。
- Anyway, *keep me informed*.
  無論如何，隨時讓我知道（這些事）。
- Well, what I propose is this. 嗯，我的建議是這樣子的。

※ 談論正事 ※

A: Is that all you wanted to see me about?

A：這就是你來找我所要談的嗎？

B: No, not quite. Now *let me get down to the main business*.

B：不，不完全是。現在讓我言歸正傳。

A: O.K.

A：好。

B: The board of directors finally agreed to set up an overseas office in New York and...

B：董事會最後一致同意在紐約設立海外公司，而且…

**

set up 設立　　overseas〔ˈovɚˈsiz〕*adj.* 海外的；國外的

❋ 討論分公司事宜 ❋

A: I wonder if there's any possibility of our setting up an overseas branch.

A：我想知道我們是否有可能成立海外分公司。

B Well, that is a difficult question and I suppose my answer is yes. Oh, it's almost noon. *Would you like to discuss it over lunch?*

B：嗯，這是個很難的問題，不過我想是有可能的。哦，快中午了，你要不要一面吃午飯，一面討論？

A: I'll be delighted to.

A：我很樂意。

B: Let's go to the cafeteria downstairs before it gets crowded.

B：讓我們在樓下自助餐廳擠滿人之前，先到那兒去。

❋ 不太確定所談論之事 ❋

A: What's happened to the new project since then?

A：從那時候起，新計劃怎麼樣了？

B: It was abandoned.

B：作罷了。

A: Was it? I thought it had just been suspended.

A：是嗎？我還以為只是暫緩而已。

---

branch〔bræntʃ〕 *n.* 分公司；分店
cafeteria〔͵kæfə'tɪrɪə,͵kæfətə'riə〕 *n.* 自助餐餐館
abandon〔ə'bændən〕 *v.* 放棄
suspend〔sə'spɛnd〕 *v.* 懸而不決；暫停；延緩

B：Well, *I'm not so sure about that*. If it had just been suspended, it should have been brought up in the meeting at least as an addendum.

B：唔，我也不太確定。如果只是暫緩而已，至少在會議中應該會附帶提出來。

A：But just think of all the money put into that project.

A：但是你想想看那計劃所花下的錢。

❋ 請對方告知詳情 ❋

A：This is all I can tell you about this project at the moment. Are you interested in it?

A：這就是目前我能告訴你的，有關這個計劃的事，你有興趣嗎？

B：Yes, very, though, I want to hear more about who else will be involved, how much money will be involved and how to raise it. *Anyway, keep me informed*.

B：有，很有興趣，不過，我想再聽聽還有誰會參與，將花多少錢，以及如何籌募資金。無論如何，隨時讓我知道（這些事）。

A：I will.

A：我會的。

❋ 提出建議 ❋

A：I'm afraid this bank won't advance the money. What shall we do?

A：恐怕這家銀行不會貸這筆款給我們，我們該怎麼辦？

---

addendum〔ə'dɛndəm〕*n.* 附加物；追加
raise〔rez〕*v.* 籌募

involve〔ɪn'vɑlv〕*v.* 包括
advance〔əd'væns〕*v.* 借貸；預付

B: Well, *what I propose is this*.
We should try a joint venture
in order to raise the necessary
fund.

B: 嗯，我的建議是這樣的。
我們該試試共同投資企
業，以籌募所需的資金。

A: That's an excellent idea. Do
you have any particular company
in mind with whom we can
enter into a joint venture
arrangement?

A: 好主意！你有沒有想到
什麼特別的公司，我們
可以開始安排共同投資
事宜的？

B: Well, there are several cam-
panies I can think of off hand.
But how about Johnson & Smith?

B: 我現在馬上就想到好幾
家公司，不過，強生暨
史密斯公司怎麼樣？

❋ 帳目不合 ❋

A: I'm afraid there is a discrep-
ancy in these figures.

A: 恐怕這些價目有不符之
處。

B: Oh, is there?

B: 噢，有嗎？

A: Yes. And there is more to it
than that.

A: 是的。而且不只是如此。

B: Oh?

B: 噢？

---

propose〔prə'poz〕v. 建議
enter into 著手；開始　　*off hand* 馬上；立即
discrepancy〔dɪ'skrɛpənsɪ〕n. 不同　　figure〔'fɪgjɚ, 'fɪgɚ〕n. 價目

A : The auditor's signature is not the same as the last time. ***Would you look into this, please***?

A : 查帳員的簽名和上回的不同。能請你調查看看嗎？

B : Certainly.

B : 當然。

❀ 公司內部人事升遷 ❀

A : Is he really quitting?

A : 他真的辭職了嗎？

B : Yes, he is. It seems he's been offered a better job by another firm.

B : 是的，他辭職了。好像是另外一家公司，提供給他一個更好的工作。

A : Is there anyone to replace him?

A : 有誰要接替他嗎？

B : Well, I just can't think of anyone offhand, but there should be somebody we'd like to promote.

B : 嗯，我無法馬上想出誰來，不過，應該有人可以提拔。

A : To take over for him?

A : 要接替他的嗎？

B : Yes. ***Please let me think it over***.

B : 是的。請讓我仔細想想看。

---

auditor〔ˈɔdɪtɚ〕 *n.* 查帳員；審計員　　signature〔ˈsɪgnətʃə〕 *n.* 簽名
look into 調查；考查　　quit〔kwɪt〕 *v.* 辭職
offhand〔ˈɔfˈhænd〕 *adv.* 即刻地　　promote〔prəˈmot〕 *v.* 升遷
take over 接管、繼任（職務）　　***think over*** 仔細考慮

✻ 裁　員 ✻

A : I'd like to talk with you.
Can you come to my office?

B : Yes, I'll be right over.

（ later ）

A : Have a seat, won't you?

B : Thank you.

A : I've been pleased with your
work, but...

B : Yes?

A : *I wish I didn't have to say
this, but* the board of directors has agreed to cut down
on the present staff.

B : I knew sooner or later this
would come.

A : 我有話要跟你說，你能
來我的辦公室嗎？

B : 好的，我馬上來。

（ 稍後 ）

A : 請坐，好嗎？

B : 謝謝。

A : 我對你的工作很滿意，
不過 …。

B : 呃？

A : 眞希望我不必跟你說這
些，但是董事會已經同
意裁員。

B : 我知道這是遲早會發生
的。

✻ 招考新職員 ✻

A : The examination is all over
and thank you for coming.

A : 考試完畢，謝謝你們來
參加。

＊＊─────────────────────────

cut down on 減少（數量等）　　　*sooner or later* 遲早；總有一天

all over 完畢

B： How soon will we know the results?

B：我們多快可以知道結果?

A： *We'll let you know as soon as we come to a decision.*

A：我們一作好決定，馬上通知你們。

B： Do you have any idea how many will be accepted?

B：你知道要錄取多少人嗎?

A： One for the editorial staff and three for the sales department.

A：一位編輯和三位門市部人員。

❋ 詢問工作條件 ❋

A： Can you tell me a bit more about the terms?

A：你能多告訴我一些關於工作條件的事嗎?

B： Certainly. What else would you like to know?

B：當然可以，你還想知道什麼?

A： What about paid holidays?

A：那給薪的休假怎麼樣呢?

B： There are three weeks of paid holidays a year.

B：一年有三個星期的給薪休假。

A： And does your company give a bonus?

A：貴公司有發給獎金嗎?

B： No. it doesn't.

B：不，沒有。

A： *Are all these terms still negotiable?*

A：這些工作條件還可以磋商嗎?

B： I'm afraid not.

B：恐怕不行。

UNIT 2

Between colleagues
同事之間

＜對話精華＞

- You see, *I got taken*! 你可知道，我被騙了。
- Well, may I *be* quite *honest with* you?
  唔，要我對你說實話嗎？
- Certainly. *I'd be happy to*.
  當然可以，我很樂意。

※ 和同事談受騙的交易 ※

A : Hey, why are you so glum this afternoon?

A：喂，你今天下午爲何這麼不快樂？

B : Oh, I don't want to talk about it!

B：噢，我不想談！

A : Come on! What happened?

A：別這樣！發生什麼事了？

B : You see, *I got taken*!

B：你可知道，我被騙了！

A : Taken?

A：被騙？

---

glum〔glʌm〕*adj*. 快快不樂的

B： Yes, we lost lots of money on this deal with an African firm.

B：是的，我們有一筆和一家非洲公司的交易，損失了很多錢。

A： Well, such things happen, you know.

A：唔，這種事有可能發生，你是知道的。

❋ 坦白指出同事所犯的錯誤 ❋

A： What do you think?

A：你覺得怎樣？

B： Well, *may I be quite honest with you*?

B：唔，要我對你說實話嗎？

A： Yes?

A：嗯嗯？

B： The way I look at it is this. Since you are not in a position to make any decision, you shouldn't have committed yourself.

B：我的看法是這樣子的。既然你不是處於決策者的地位，你就不應該作承諾。

❋ 樂意幫忙同事 ❋

A： Mr. Chen, will you do me a favor?

A：陳先生，能幫我一個忙嗎？

---

be honest with 坦白的透露…；對…說老實話
in a position to 有資格；處於能做（某事的）地位
commit oneself 涉入（危險的事）；〔因承諾而〕受約束

B : Yes, if I can. What do you want me to do?

B：好的，如果我能幫得上忙。你要我做什麼呢？

A : Could you help me locate this Taiwan friend of mine?

A：你能幫我找這個台灣朋友嗎？

B : *Certainly. I'd be happy to.*

B：當然可以，我很樂意。

※ 邀同事共進晚餐 ※

A : Say, how about joining me for dinner somewhere after we get through with this?

A：喂，辦完這事之後，和我一起找個地方共進晚餐如何？

B : That's a superb idea! In that case, why don't we invite Mr. Chen to come with us?

B：眞是好主意！如果那樣的話，我們何不邀陳先生一起去？

A : I wish I could. *He's left for the day.*

A：我希望可以。不過他已經走了。

B : That's too bad.

B：眞不巧。

---

locate〔loˊket〕v. 尋出～的位置   *get through with* 完成；結束

UNIT 3

Handling the complaints of a customer
處理客戶的抱怨

> ～～～〈對話精華〉～～～
>
> · The **home office** asked me **to drop in and see you**.
>   總公司要我 前來拜訪你。
>
> · **I'll want to take a look**, of course. 我當然想看看。
>
> · You're right. **A mistake has been made**.
>   你說得沒錯，是出了一點差錯。

※ 客戶表示上批貨不合標準 ※

A : Mr. Chen, we have a problem.

A : 陳先生，我們有個問題。

B : With what ?

B : 哪方面的問題？

A : The material you sent us on the last order.

A : 有關你們上批貨料的問題。

B : What's the problem ?

B : 問題在哪？

A : Most of the units weren't up to your usual standards.

A : 大部分的原件，不合你們平常的標準。

❈ 客戶表示上批貨裝錯了 ❈

A : Mr. Johnson, you wanted to see me?

A : 強森先生，你要見我嗎?

B : Yes. There was a problem with your last shipment.

B : 是的。你們上批貨有個問題。

A : Really? *I was sure everything was all right with that shipment*.

A : 眞的嗎？我原以爲該批貨一切都沒問題。

B : We thought so, too, until we opened the shipping crates.

B : 打開裝貨的板條箱之前，我們也一直這麼想。

A : What was wrong?

A : 出了什麼差錯?

B : The crates were labeled A-3.

B : 板條箱貼著A-3的標籤。

A   A-3? That's just what you ordered.

A : A-3? 那正是你們訂購的。

B : Right. We ordered A-3's, but the box contained A-1's. We can't use those at all.

B : 沒錯。我們訂的是A-3的貨，但盒子內裝的是A-1的貨。這些我們根本不能用。

❈ 客戶表示有所不滿 ❈

A : Hello, Mr. Dowler. How's everything?

A : 你好，多勒先生。一切好嗎?

---

crate〔kret〕*n.* 板條箱　　label〔'lebḷ〕*v.* 貼標籤於

B： I'm glad you asked.

A： Oh?

B： Yes. We have a complaint to make.

A： Really? *I'm sorry to hear that.*

B：我很高興你有此一問。

A：喔?

B：嗯。我們有不滿的事要說

A：眞的嗎?聽到這種事眞是抱歉。

※ 請客戶說明抱怨的原因 ※

A： I'm afraid I have a complaint.

B： About your last order?

A： That's right.

B： *Please tell me about it.*

A：恐怕我有不滿的事。

B：有關你們上次訂的貨嗎?

A：沒錯。

B：請講給我聽聽。

※ 被派來處理客戶的抱怨 ※

A： *The home office asked me to drop in and see you.*

B： Yes. I contacted them some time ago.

A： They said you have a complaint.

B： That's right.

A： What's the nature of the problem?

A：總公司要我前來拜訪你。

B：是啊。我前些時候跟他們聯絡過。

A：他們說你有所不滿。

B：不錯。

A：是哪方面的問題?

B : We can't use most of the material you sent us on the last shipment.

B：上批貨的材料，大部分我們都不能用。

❀ 表示願意和客戶到工廠調查問題所在 ❀

A : Do you have time to go out to our New Jersey factory with us ?

A：你有時間一起去我們的紐澤西廠嗎？

B : Sure. Why do you want to go out there ?

B：當然有。你們爲什麼要到那兒去呢？

A : We're having a problem with the last shipment you sent us.

A：你們上次送來的貨有了問題。

B : *I'll want to take a look, of course*. When do you want to go ?

B：我當然想看看。你們什麼時候要去？

A : How about next Tuesday ?

A：下禮拜二怎樣？

B : That's fine. Let's set it up for next Tuesday.

B：好啊。我們就排定在下禮拜二。

❀ 答應客戶儘快送去替換品 ❀

A : Well, what's your opinion ?

A：嗯，你有什麼意見？

B : You're right. *A mistake has been made*.

B：你說的沒錯。是出了一點差錯。

A : What are you going to do about it?

A：你打算怎麼辦？

B : We'll send you a replacement shipment right away.

B：我們會立刻替你們送來替換品。

A : Will it take long? We really need this material.

A：這要花很久的時間嗎？我們急需這種材料。

B : I'll have them rush it right through for you.

B：我會請他們火速送來。

Editorial Staff

- ●企劃・編著／王慈嫺
- ●校訂
    葉淑霞・武藍蕙・賴明雪・陳志忠・湯碧秋
    陳威如・林　婷
- ●校閱
    Mark Pengra・Lois M. Findler
    John H. Voelker・Michael Hardy
- ●封面設計／唐　旻
- ●版面設計／張鳳儀
- ●版面構成／謝淑敏・黃春蓮・蘇翠鳳
- ●打字
    黃淑貞・倪秀梅・蘇淑玲・吳秋香
    洪桂美・徐湘君
- ●校對
    王慶銘・陳佳麗・林韶慧・葉美利・李南施
    陳瑠琍・王之瑋・楊秀娟・邱蔚獎・楊秋梅

＜＝＝＝＞ 本書另附有高品質錄音帶四捲500元，由
美籍電台播音員錄音，配合學習，效果更佳。

商用基礎會話

編　　著 / 王 慈 嫻

發 行 所 / 學習出版有限公司　　　☎ (02) 2704-5525

郵 撥 帳 號 / 0512727-2 學習出版社帳戶

登 記 證 / 局版台業 2179 號

印 刷 所 / 裕強彩色印刷有限公司

台 北 門 市 / 台北市許昌街 10 號 2 F　　☎ (02) 2331-4060・2331-9209

台 中 門 市 / 台中市綠川東街 32 號 8 F 23 室　　☎ (04) 2223-2838

台灣總經銷 / 紅螞蟻圖書有限公司　　☎ (02) 2795-3656

美國總經銷 / Evergreen Book Store　　☎ (818) 2813622

本公司網址　www.learnbook.com.tw

電 子 郵 件　learnbook@learnbook.com.tw

售價：新台幣一百五十元正

2003 年 9 月 1 日一版六刷

ISBN 957-519-012-2